D0402004

A
Woman
of
Strength

Pg 125/ch 14

Women of Confidence

SERIES

Reclaim Your Past,
Seize Your Present,
and Secure Your Future

NEVA COYLE

SERVANT PUBLICATIONS
ANN ARBOR, MICHIGAN

Vine Books is an imprint of Servant Publications especially designed
to serve evangelical Christians.

Published by Servant Publications
P.O. Box 8617
Ann Arbor, Michigan 48107

97 98 99 00 10 9 8 7 6 5 4 3 2

Printed in the United States of America
ISBN 1-56955-036-0

LIBRARY OF CONGRESS CATALOGING-IN-PUBLICATION DATA

Coyle, Neva
    A woman of strength : reclaim your past, seize your present, and secure
your future / by Neva Coyle.
        p. cm. — (Women of confidence series ; 2)
    Includes bibliographical references.
    ISBN 1-56955-036-0
    1. Christian women—Religious life. I. Title. II. Series.
BV4527.C695   1997
248.8'43—dc21   97-24505
                                                        CIP

This book is dedicated to my friend and mentor,

Barbara Tollefson.

Contents

Introduction

If I were to say, "Now there goes a *really strong* woman," would a certain name or face come to mind? On the other hand, if I were to suggest, "Now there is a real *woman of strength*," would a different name or face occur to you?

I know strong women and I know women of strength—and you probably do, too. Both are role models from which we learn, and, in many cases, emulate. But do we actually have any choice in the matter or are we destined or naturally bent to become either one or the other? How do I want to be remembered, as a *strong woman* who rides roughshod over others or as a *woman of deep inner strength* who walks with grace through life? That question sent me searching for answers.

What makes the difference between these women? Why does one send everyone in her presence scurrying toward the nearest exit while another draws people to her? Why does one desperately need to control and the other perfectly content and fulfilled being an encourager and facilitator? Is it simply a matter of personality or personal style? Or, is it something more—something we can learn? Something we can grow into?

Perhaps you would like to feel more effective, to be liberated from your past or just not feel so weak anymore. Perhaps you've been victimized and are tired of feeling used. Maybe you're feeling burned out but don't know how to stop being responsible for everything and everyone.

If you're one of those special, growing women who long for strength, who desire to be more capable or victorious when life throws them a curve, then this book is for you. It will help you in your effort to be more decisive without being overbearing. It will encourage you to look beyond your limitations to realize that you can be more than you are in your present experience. It will help you know how to use the pain of your past to become what you long to be.

This book is purposely designed to help you become a *woman of strength* and to help you avoid the pitfalls of becoming a *strong woman*. It will also help you identify what you are now, and show you where you need to make some corrections in your course.

I believe that you and I can personally realize what it means to be a woman of purpose and destiny, of courage as well as contentment, and to grow into women of godly character and strength. And, if you recognize yourself as a *strong woman,* this book will help you identify ways in which you can change those strong characteristics into *strengths.*

Which do you prefer to be? A strong woman or a woman of strength? The challenging decision is right here in front of you. It's not too late to change. The choice to do so is yours. The door of opportunity is wide open. Let this book be your guide.

In the first section of this book, we will lay the groundwork and do some planning as if we were going on a tour or a guided trip. As with every trip, some preplanning is necessary if the road ahead is to be navigated successfully and without unfortunate incidents or delay.

In the second part of the book, we will actually begin our journey together. At the end of each chapter there will be checkpoints. When you take a road trip, you have to stop, refuel, rest, or take a break just to walk around a bit. However, the checkpoints in this book are to give you "thinking and processing" breaks. These checkpoints are questions designed to let you respond to what you have just read, help you see how far you've come, or prepare you for what's ahead.

If you are using this book as a group study, these checkpoint questions will be a good springboard for discussion.

✓ Checkpoint:

When you read, "Now there goes a *really strong* woman," what face or name came to mind?

When you read, "Now there is a real *woman of strength*," what different name or face occurred to you?

What are the differences between these two women? Who are you most like?

Which of these women do you most want to be like? Why?

Part One

Getting Ready

1

You Are Where?

I parked my car in the only space I could find. I took note of how far it was to the entrance of the mall and heaved a big sigh. Resigning ourselves to the prospect that anything we bought we would have to lug back to the car, my shopping companion and I headed toward the largest outlet shopping mall in the state of California. Once inside, I looked for the nearest floor directory. Picking up the mall brochure, I put a check mark by every store that interested me and then referred to the large floor directory in front of me.

"You Are Here"

I found the little box marked "X" down on one distant corner. "Oh, no!" I moaned repeatedly as I located every store on my list. "Everything's so far from here! I don't want to be *here*," I said to my friend, "I want to be *there!*" I pointed to a more centralized location.

"Well, you're not *there*," she said. "You're *here*, and as long as you stand here moaning, you'll never be close to *there*." She studied the map closely. "One good thing," she said shrugging into a better mood, "at least we know where we are, and how to get there from here."

How often I have looked at where I want to be compared to where I am and simply moaned in distress or even disgust. Whether it's circumstantial, spiritual, or personal goals I'd like to achieve, I am often overwhelmed when I see how far I have to go.

How about you? If you were to look at the map of your life (as if it were a shopping mall directory), and then locate the "You Are Here" little box marked ✖, would you say, "Yep! It's exactly where I want to be—I'm exactly where I planned to be at this time in my life"? If so, then you might as well pass this book on to a friend. But if, like me, you would say, "I'm not where or what I want to be yet," then keep reading.

Whether you find you are too weak or too strong, whether people are leaving tire tracks across your face or if you are making tracks on the faces of others, you can change. Rest assured that there are women right around you also dissatisfied with who and what they have become or where they are headed if they don't make course corrections. Even if you are certain you're being manipulated by everyone in your life, or know that you are the manipulator, you can change and so can your life.

The overburdened and the overachiever alike can become women of strength. For the perpetual victim and for the one who is overbearing, there is promise of change. If a place of inner strength and depth of character is where you want to get to from here ✖, come along with me and the many women who will be reading this book. We know there is more to life than our present experience. Certainly we can become more capable, taste victory more often, and make healthier decisions. Without a doubt we can *grow* there from here, no matter where *here* happens to be.

But it won't happen overnight. It's a growth process, a personal journey. It's a pathway we will travel together. What's more, here is a good place and today is a good time to begin. Ready?

Getting Our Bearings

If you were standing at the "mall directory" of your life, would you have the courage to spot the "You Are Here" box marked "X"? It's important. You see, to get where you want to be, you have to know two things: your destination and your starting place.

When you're mapping out a course of travel and you want to get to Indianapolis, it's imperative that you know if you're starting from Los Angeles or Minneapolis. In the same way, if you want to get to *there* in life from *here*, both points—departure and destination—have to be known.

So let's begin. Let's muster the courage to find our life's "You Are Here" ✖ icon. Let's choose to be specific and begin with a prayer. Use these words to help you get started, then speak to God from your heart.

Dear Heavenly Father, I'm not satisfied with the present status of my life. Help me change,
in my relationship with …
in how I make excuses for …
in the way I handle …
my attitudes toward …
the continued pain of …
my emotional response to …

in my lack of ability to …
my devotional life, because …
I want better control of my …
I need more …
please help me …
show me where I'm wrong in …
help me open my heart to …
I need more strength in …

I want more, dear God, more of what you have destined for me to become. I want your purpose for my life and my character. I want to become a true woman of God, a genuine woman of strength. I trust you, Father, to help me grow into a woman of strength. I know that with your help, I can grow there from here. In Jesus' name, amen.

Your courageous prayer is not that much different from the brave words found in Psalms 139:23-24: *Search me, O God, and know my heart; test me and know my anxious thoughts. See if there is any offensive way in me, and lead me in the way everlasting.*

Now that's spotting the "X," letting God's Holy Spirit illumine your inner self as if with fluorescent highlighter, "You Are Here." ✖ And what if it's miles from where you and he want you to be? You can *grow* there from here. It's not my promise—but his! Think of God saying to you the words of Isaiah 45:2-3:

> I will go before you and will level the mountains; I will break
> down gates of bronze and cut through bars of iron.
> I will give you the treasures of darkness,
> riches stored in secret places,
> so that you may know that I am the LORD,
> the God of Israel, who summons you by name.

He has your itinerary all planned. Pack your bags, you're on your way. You are destined to become a woman of strength. What is your choice?

✓ Checkpoint:

"You Are Here" but you have no doubt that God wants you to grow to a new level of confidence in him. Write out a description of the kind of woman you want to become.

In your opinion, how far are you from your destination? No course has yet been made clear, though we will see one in the chapters that follow.

What is the one main obstacle in your life that prevents you from becoming all you want to be in Christ?

How can you take strength and hope from Isaiah 45:2-3?

2

"How'd I Get Here, Anyway?"

What keeps me from being the woman of strength I'd like to be? Have you ever asked yourself that question before? I have, many times. My progress often seems slow. Other times it's even worse and I feel as if I'm standing still in my growth toward God's best for me. And, saddest of all, there are actually times when I sense I'm regressing, not progressing. It can be downright discouraging! However, I'm not one for making defeat a career, and eventually I collect myself enough to search prayerfully and carefully for answers. A good place to begin is by asking, "Who am I, anyway?"

As a novelist, I consider every person a story, every life a book. I'm an unfinished volume, and so are you. In writing a novel, the writer must know every character at a depth in direct proportion to his importance to the story. The central characters must be known from their very beginning—their background, their psychological profile, their relationship with Christ, and even their favorite foods and colors. This gives them depth and believability. Since you and I are each main characters in the individual volumes of our own lives, let's explore together what makes us uniquely us.

Each of us is born. We know that, but our conception of the

circumstances of our very beginnings has a bearing on who we become. Who do you see you are from the circumstances surrounding your moment of conception? Do you perceive yourself as an accident? An unplanned or unwanted child? Wanted and welcomed? Were you an interruption to your parents or a blessing? And who defines that?

Let me tell you this: no matter what anyone has ever said, hinted, or caused you to feel, God planned, first of all, that you have life.[1] He also planned that your life be trademarked with abundance.[2] Whether or not your earthly parents planned for your birth, God did. He's glad you're here. He only used your parents to give you the genetic structure he planned for you.

But our uniqueness is more than just than a genetic beginning. Each of us was born into a particular culture. Women of varying ethnic origins are reading this book right along with you, and those women are just as deeply ingrained in their ethnicity as you are in yours. Our cultures play an important role both in helping us become what we will be, and also in limiting what we become. Your culture helped you get to the little ✖—you are *here* ✖ partly because of your culture. Whether you were humble and disadvantaged or born into privilege, whether you were born into a Christian or a completely secular environment, your culture has helped put you *here*. Sometimes, if we're not careful, our culture can be an obstacle to growing on from here.

Not only are we each given to certain parents and socialized into a particular culture, we are also products of our own historical period. For example, I am a Baby Boomer. Raised in the forties and fifties, then married in the early sixties—I have a vastly different perspective of life than my parents, who were born in 1916.

They married in the mid-nineteen thirties during a very depressed period of our nation's history. I heard all their stories of hard times—extended families living together to save money and how hard it was to get a job. That was my parents' experience, but it wasn't mine. I have been influenced by *my* historical period. They lived through World Wars I and II. I vaguely remember the Korean War. I was most impacted by our military involvement in Vietnam. I passed on the stories of the Vietnam War times to my own children, who were impacted very little by them because, after all, my children are children of the seventies and eighties, a far different world than my formative years.

It's true: my historical setting, my background, and the world around me have helped shape me into who I am. Not only emotionally and spiritually, but even politically. This is part of how I got *here*.

Socioeconomic factors have also helped shape my life, as they have yours. Opportunities, education, and even my personal value as described by contemporary society have all determined how I came to be where I am at this very moment. Circumstances, both those of my own doing and those not, have also directed or even dictated my pathway to *here*.

When we look toward growing on from *here* ✖ into women of strength, it will be with an appreciative glance over our shoulders. We must understand that life isn't simply a series of decisions or choices, it is also a history of influence—sometimes good, sometimes not; sometimes a help, sometimes a hindrance. But believe me, an understanding of where we've come from is an invaluable resource and source of insight and information when you desire to grow on with your life.

Identify Areas of Needed Growth

If you were to identify one major area in which you need to grow—one personal, emotional, or spiritual destination—could you also identify the obstacles that stand between you and your goal? Would a glance over your shoulder into your beginnings, culture, or the condition of current times give you a clue? Have any of those factors contributed in any way to boundaries—real or perceived—that could be hindering you? In other words, could the same factors that have forced or guided you to *here* be keeping you *here*? If so, then becoming a woman of strength also means you will learn to be an overcomer.

Have others limited you or put boundaries in your life that you'd like lifted? Do circumstances dictate that you have to be stuck *here* when you'd really like to grow *there*? Then it's time to move on, even if it's only on the inside for the moment. Begin by giving yourself permission to hope that you can grow *there* from *here* ✖ .

And what about the limitations you have put on yourself? Take another glance over your shoulder. You could still be carrying lies about your worth, your intelligence, or your value from your beginning or culture. You could be defining yourself by unhappy events or personal history. If so, it's time to move on. You've got so much to gain by growing from *here* to *there*. Becoming a woman of strength is your destiny now. You've got big shoes to fill, and guess what, they're yours.

Opening the Gate to Growth

Some women I talked to about this subject believed they already were women of strength. However, in talking to them, I had a hunch I was talking to "strong" women. Is there a difference? We know there is. "Strong" is *not* what I want to be. I'd much rather be a woman of strength.

In the next chapter, let's take a look at a woman of strength from Scripture. Abigail was an admirable woman of great inner strength, who walked in wisdom and grace.

✓ Checkpoint:

If you think of yourself as an unfinished book, what would the title most likely be?

Does that title reflect where you've come from or where you want to *grow* to?

Identify one major area in your life in which you need to grow.

If God were to remove the obstacles that kept growth from happening in you, what do you think he'd start with and what changes would you see begin to happen in your life?

What resistance inside of you would God run into if he began to *grow* you into a woman of strength?

3

Abigail–A Woman of Strength

"What is it?" Abigail asked when she heard the commotion in the next room.

"It's one of the men ... " the servant girl tried to explain.

"Madam," a ruddy man said as he brushed by the girl, "it's your husband." He bowed low before her. "I'm afraid he's ... "

"Go on," Abigail urged. "What's Nabal done this time?"

"He's insulted David—*David*," the man answered.

"David?" Abigail's hand flew involuntarily to her long, slender throat. "Go on, tell me."

"David sent messengers from the desert to give our master, Nabal, his greetings, but our master hurled insults at them. These men were very good to us. They did not mistreat us, and the whole time we were out in the fields near them nothing was missing. Night and day they were like a wall around us. They protected us all the time we were herding our sheep. Please see what you can do to appease David, because disaster is hanging over our master and all of us. Nabal is such a wicked man that no one can talk to him."[1]

Abigail closed her eyes, trying to shut out the awful truth. Nabal's evil doings could have far-reaching implications. Taking a deep breath she gathered as much courage as she could. She needed strength to deal with this situation. It wasn't the first time she'd been put in this position by her surly and foolish husband. How could she make David understand?

Abigail knew the stories circulating about David. She knew how God's hand had rested on him again and again. He'd be king before long. Many already looked at him as if he were. Nabal was a fool. David was angry and his anger was justified. Revenge was certain. She must make David see he mustn't waste his time on someone as trivial as Nabal.

The servant girl's fear-filled, urgent whisper interrupted her thoughts. "What are you going to do? Surely you don't plan to … Wait, Mistress Abigail, your husband, I beg forgiveness for what I'm about to say—but he isn't worth it. Don't put yourself in danger because of him."

"We're already in danger because of him," Abigail answered calmly. "But there's much at stake here. Hurry now, there's not a moment to lose."

Quickly, she made her decisions. She took two hundred loaves of bread, two skins of wine, five dressed sheep, five sacks of roasted grain, a hundred cakes of raisins, and two hundred cakes of pressed figs, and loaded them on donkeys. Then she told her servants, "Go ahead; I'll follow you." She told Nabal nothing.

Abigail carefully planned what she would say to David. Somehow she'd have to make him understand. After all God had done for him, an act of revenge against Nabal, even though justified, could lead David away from God's plan. It might sear his conscience—harden his heart. Intuitively, she knew she must get to David before he got to Nabal. Surely God would not fail to help her now. God's plan and purposes were hanging in the balance.

She must reach David in time. Abigail stepped decisively forward in wisdom's shining moment.

As she came riding her donkey into a mountain ravine, she saw David and his men descending toward her. She could hear his angry voice even from this distance.

"It's been a useless endeavor—all my watching over this fellow's property so that nothing of his was missing. He has paid me back evil for good. May God deal severely with me, if I leave alive one male of all who belong to him!" The words were barely out of David's mouth when he saw her.

Quickly, Abigail got off her donkey and bowed down before David with her face to the ground. With careful attention to protocol and David's position, she humbled herself in the dust at his feet. Her enormous responsibility weighed heavily on her slim shoulders. She forced herself to be calm.

"My lord," she said bravely, "let the blame be on me alone. Please let your servant speak to you; hear what your servant has to say. May my lord pay no attention to that wicked man, Nabal. His name is Fool, and he is just like his name. Folly goes with him. But as for me, your servant, I did not see the men you sent.

"Now since the Lord has kept you, my master, from bloodshed and from avenging yourself with your own hands, as surely as the Lord lives and as you live, may your enemies and all who intend to harm my master be like Nabal. And let this gift, which your servant has brought, be given to the men who follow you. Please forgive your servant, Nabal's, offense, for the Lord will certainly make a lasting dynasty for my master, because he fights the Lord's battles. Let no wrongdoing be found in you as long as you live. Even though someone is pursuing you to take your life, the life of my master will be bound securely in the bundle of the living by the

Lord your God. But the lives of your enemies he will hurl away as from the pocket of a sling. When the Lord has done for you every good thing he promised concerning you and has appointed you leader over Israel, my master will not have on his conscience the staggering burden of needless bloodshed nor of having avenged himself. And when the Lord has brought my master success," her heartbeat quickened, "remember your servant."

Her message to David was loud and clear: *Don't take things into your own hands. Why risk everything God has given you and that which he has promised yet to give you for a moment of revenge on a fool?* What courage she had! What strength!

David admired Abigail and listened to her wise words of advice. And while she saved David from doing himself great harm, she released her husband to be dealt with by God. The Bible tells us that when Nabal heard what she had done, he had a stroke and died a few days later. Before long, David sent for the widowed Abigail and made her his wife.

Abigail revealed deep inner character. She was indeed a woman of strength. Her example of wisdom and great character leaves a rich legacy of womanhood that can only be embraced and realized by those women who would put God and his will before themselves and their own will. Would you or I dare to have the courage and humility to put his purposes first?

✓ Checkpoint:

How do the lessons of Abigail relate to the definitive *woman of strength* you identified at the end of the introductory chapter?

Think of a definite circumstance when you purposely put God and his will before your own. Be specific.

How much courage did that take?

What were the positive results?

4

Who Are They, These Women of Strength?

A lthough we don't often think about it, there are plenty of negative role models in Scripture.[1] Women like Jezebel, who was savage, relentless, proud, and strong-minded. A gifted woman, Jezebel prostituted all her gifts for the furtherance of evil. In the execution of her foul schemes, her misdirected talents became a curse. She was a persuasive woman whose influence was wrongly directed, a resolute woman who used her strength to destroy the king and her own children and to pollute the life of a nation.

Herodias is the New Testament counterpart of the Old Testament Jezebel. Both women were married to strong, evil men who were perhaps even stronger and lower in their evil natures than their wives. And who could overlook the negative role model in Delilah? She used her strong seductive powers to manipulate, domineer, and destroy Samson. She betrayed him for a price.

Biblical Examples of Women of Strength

Standing in sharp contrast to these women are the godly women of the Bible who show us the pathway and the inner character of women of strength. In the Old Testament we see qualities of faith in the strength of Jochebed, the mother of Moses, who defied death, and then quietly trusted God to protect her son as she set him afloat in a crocodile-infested river. This woman of strength managed to keep quiet the fact that she was Moses' birth mother as God orchestrated his adoption into the house of Pharaoh.

Deborah, daring and dynamic in leadership, led her entire nation into moral purification. She shows us character of strength through total dedication to God. A prophetess, ruler, warrior, and poetess—no character in the Old Testament stands out in bolder relief than this "mother in Israel."

Esther's story shows us qualities of a woman of strength in her courage and great personal risk. She approached her husband, the king, uninvited, as God's instrument of intervention for the good of his people, while Vashhti, Esther's predecessor refused her husband's request to perform lewd acts, and stood for right.

Mary, the mother of Jesus, shows us strength in courage, trust, and obedience. She risked her reputation and the love of her betrothed Joseph to cooperate with God in his most unusual and unexpected request.

Anna, widowed after only seven years of a childless marriage, shows us her strength through commitment and faithfulness. Serving tirelessly in fasting and prayer in the temple, Anna prophesied the appearance of the Messiah. What a thrill it must have been to hold him in her arms at last! Surely she looked upon his divine baby face through sharp spiritual, but declining physical, eyesight.

Phoebe shows us her great strength in trustworthiness. She was entrusted to carry the entire book of Romans to the Christians in Rome when Paul couldn't go himself. In a culture where a woman didn't even show her face, or go anywhere alone, to Phoebe was given the task of delivering the plan of salvation still used today by altar workers and evangelists.

Rizpah serves as an example of strength because of her loving care of the dead. The widow of Zarephath generously gave bread to the hungry. Dorcas' strength of character was demonstrated in her care of widows and her clothing of the poor. Martha was the epitome of gracious hospitality, and Mary is still known for her sacrifice of the box of fragrant ointment she broke to anoint the feet of Jesus.

All these women and many more, leave for us a rich heritage of strength—a deep inner character hallmarked by service, sacrifice, and devotion. They leave us a legacy of commitment and perseverance, and examples of strong faith, trust, and obedience. These are role models much needed in our contemporary Christian culture. These are the lifestyles of the rich in spirit. These are paradigms of godly women who show us how to sow our own seeds of faith and character for a plentiful harvest of fruitfulness in Christ's kingdom.

I pray that we are ready to become women of strength, that you and I are willing to look away from our own interests and personal agendas long enough to seek out the common thread of godly character that weaves through the lives and examples left to us by these women. These admirable members of a sisterhood of strength have left us a well-worn path to follow. This is a legacy we are responsible to leave to other women yet unborn. In our walk through this world in this particular period of history, let us pledge to leave a heritage worth knowing and living. Others have, and we can, too.

Personal Heroes and Women of Strength

In the pages of church history and of more modern times, we find several examples of women who dared to carry on the legacy of strength. Teresa of Avila, for example, was a woman who lived in the sixteenth century. Her entire life's goal was to live and be like Christ. David Hazard writes of her:

> So deep was her desire to walk the path of her Lord's humility, that she could not be provoked to speak a word in her own defense—not even when the Inquisition ordered that both Teresa and her writings be seized "for examination."[2]

Teresa, a lone young woman trying to live a pure faith, comes under vicious attack by the very institution she loves. She submits herself, body, and soul, to their intense pressure and scrutiny and, despite all that, she spearheads a vast spiritual revival. If Teresa were alive today, agents would be offering her film contracts.

Teresa of Avila leaves for us a legacy of strength, strength in humility. "God calls us to come to him," Hazard concludes in his book, "and if we want to walk in his fellowship, we must stop seeking our worth, comfort, and security in anything else." Simple humility—what glorious strength.

One of my personal heroines is Amy Carmichael. As a young woman, Carmichael battled and overcame a desire central to the emotional well-being of almost every woman. She conquered her desire for husband and family and embarked on a life of total devotion to God's call with her life unencumbered by familial responsibility and duty. As a single woman she was mobile and found herself more flexible as the Spirit of God moved and directed her life into several areas and ministries in Asia. Carmichael founded the Dohnavur Fellowship in India, which rescued, protected, and parented young girls and boys given to the temple for prostitution. Though she left home in her early twenties, she never returned for a furlough, fund-raising event, or missions convention. She simply stayed put in India and made ministry her life. Carmichael's biographer, Elisabeth Elliot, records that she was a woman with a fragile and tender heart.[3] And though she never physically gave birth to a child of her own, she took in the abandoned children of many, becoming a true "mother" of countless children.

Amy Carmichael was a most outstanding woman of strength and character. She was totally faithful and trustworthy in her dedication and commitment to God's call on her life. A poetess who has stirred my heart with words of encouragement and hope, she revealed herself as a woman whose deepest inner self was open to God.

Women through the centuries have left us mile markers of the true character of women of strength. Jesse Penn-Lewis illuminates our pathway to strength through her books, Mother Teresa through her tireless work of a self-sacrificing life of loving touch, and Rosalind Rinker in her practical approach to prayer.

One of my very favorite women of strength is Catherine Marshall. None of the women I have written about so far has impacted me personally as much as this beloved woman. I was first acquainted with her through her writing, where she taught me tenderly to look beyond myself for something more. I devoured every one of her books that I could get my hands on. Often I read through them in one sitting. My copies of her books are marked with highlighters and underlined in pen. I filled the margins with little notes of personal response and application.

Imagine my excitement when one day in Minneapolis I got to shake Catherine Marshall's hand—my heroine had skin! I watched with eagerness and respect as she unhurriedly autographed several books for people standing quietly in an almost unending line. Taking time to make eye contact with each one, she made everyone feel as special to her as she was to them. I'll never forget the impression she made on me when she said she had read one of my books and even told me her favorite part, how it helped her, then thanked me for writing it. Catherine Marshall demonstrated the strength of an encourager. A busy, sought-after woman, she took the time to encourage this brand new writer on a pathway she herself had traveled long before.

Many of our contemporaries are great women of strength. Corrie ten Boom, Ruth Graham, Joni Eareskon Tada, Ann Kiemel Anderson, Anna Hayford—all are women who have learned the secret of becoming women of strength. They have not only received the legacy, but have, and are, still passing it on to women like you and me.

Nancy A. Hardesty could be writing about my personal heroines when she writes:

> Central to all these women's lives was *and is* their love for God, their devotion to Christ, and their compassion to others. Love. Christ commanded that we love God with all our heart. These women did *and do* so, often with an intensity and selflessness that affronts us in the post-Freudian, narcissistic twentieth century. We have forgotten how to love God wholeheartedly; we have become fearful of the consequences of such a commitment. (italics mine)[4]

In my view, we have become weak women with strong personalities driven by personal, fleshly appetites. That way of living is not enough for me. How about you? I believe we can become women of strength. We can *grow* there from *here*, wherever and whatever that means to each of us. With such godly examples and the availability of such worthy mentors right around us, we, too, can be women of strength. Let's identify what characteristics determine and define women of strength.

✓ Checkpoint:

"Central to all these women's lives was *and is* their love for God, their devotion to Christ, and their compassion to others" (italics mine, Nancy A. Hardesty). Using this statement as your definition, make a list of all the women of strength you know or admire.

How can you make these women your personal heroines and role models?

If you were to use these women as role models for your own growth, what are some of the changes you could expect to make?

5

The Stuff of Which Women of Strength Are Made

I'm dissatisfied. I'm tired of being too weak sometimes, too strong other times, and on other occasions, not sure whether to be weak or strong. Sometimes I say and do exactly the opposite of what I want to say or do. Furthermore, I'm sick of second-guessing myself. I have moments when I am directly aware of how my own prayerlessness cripples me, and how the neglect of God's Word leaves me open to being battered by life. And, I want more. To be more. When it's all said and done, I want to leave more than weakness behind when I die.

No matter how far I've come, no matter what I have accomplished, I want to change. I want an insatiable appetite for God and what I can be in him. I also want to plumb the depths of what he can be in me. I want his strength. I want to be his woman of strength.

How about you? Isn't this what you really want to be? Do you want to know for sure that your own emotional and spiritual development and your maturity are right on track, on target with what he wants for you?

Characteristics of Women of Strength

Let's look at the lives and legacies of women of strength and examine several of their key inner characteristics.

Women of strength carry an inward inner quality of quiet trust.

If we look closely, we will see that Jochebed's strength was her quiet trust in God. Not just trust, but *quiet* trust. The depth of her trust motivated a calculated risk. If God hadn't come through for her, Jochebed would not only have paid with Moses' life, but probably her own. She couldn't tell anyone, except for Miriam and Aaron, what she was doing. She kept her plan safely behind closed doors. Only God knew for sure the outcome—he was directing her. Her responsibility? To quietly trust.

How many times have I spilled out my fears, misgivings, and troubles, only to end the conversation with words like, "But I'm trusting God in this"? Is that *quiet* trust? My goal is to become so strong in God that I do trust him no matter what my circumstances may be. I want to *immediately* respond in trust, not trouble.

Women of strength pursue total dedication to God.

Deborah demonstrates this characteristic. She was living in a man's world, smack dab in the middle of a culture that hardly recognized the value, worth, and dignity of women at all. She wasn't dedicated to the cause of all women everywhere, nor did she see herself as a pioneer in a "women's movement." Her dedication was on a much higher plane than that. She was dedicated totally to God.

It's so much easier to dedicate myself to a cause; to whip up enthusiasm in my friends; to recruit others to join me and support me in my cause rather than to totally dedicate myself to God. However, dedication to God gives women strength, no matter what others do. The difficult aspect of developing dedication is that it is often done in solitude. Support of friends and family? Don't count on it. Total dedication to God is a personal, solitary act of devotion and commitment.

Women of strength are willing to take a personal risk.

With six simple words bolstering her, Queen Esther makes her courageous move: "For such a time as this ..."[1] How those words must have rung in her heart as she dared defend the cause of God's people and to preserve his purpose for them. Can you and I say that we have that kind of conviction-based courage? How long has it been since you felt the strength that comes from knowing without a doubt that even though what you were about to do or say could cost you dearly, you have a divinely driven sense of purpose? Your life may not have been hanging in the balance as Esther's was, but maybe the acceptance of your peers at work was, or maybe your reputation with your friends, or your standing in the church.

A woman of strength knows to take the time to prepare herself as Esther did. She goes into seclusion for a season if necessary, to gather the strength of God's power to perform what he requires. God's power gives her the confidence to take the risks necessary to move in his will.

Women of strength understand righteous refusal.

It's true, there are husbands, even Christian husbands, who ask more of their wives than is appropriate or even decent. Vashti's husband was one of those. What her husband asked of her was far beyond his right as her husband. Vashti refused to expose herself to his friends to bolster his ego. And so she lost her position as queen.

How far are you and I willing *not* to go? Women of strength have a godly self-respect that will eventually collide with the permissive, immoral decadence of our day. I guarantee it. A situation will someday arise in your life and in mine that will require righteous refusal. There will come a situation at work or with a neighbor, or even someone at church where we will have to righteously refuse. There will come a time of testing that tempts us to go beyond the limits. There will come a time to take a stand and quietly, discreetly refuse.

Women of strength trust and obey God, no matter what.

With everything on the line—her very reputation to preserve—Mary said "yes" to God. She had no mentor to help her with this. No one else had ever been asked to do what God was asking her. Mary didn't consider the price of submitting to God's will too high.

Do you respond with such trust in your obedience? Do I? The question probes me deeply. How many times have you and I known what God was asking, but responded with, "Yes, but what about … ?" What am I willing to sacrifice to see God's will fully demonstrated in my life? Possessions? Habits? Opinions? Schedule? Is there anything I hold so tightly that he can't lay claim on my entire heart? If we are ever to become true women of strength, we have to grow to a place in our trust that nothing, absolutely nothing he asks of us will ever be denied him.

We know, of course, that what God asks of us, while personally costly, is never irrational. All through the Bible we see that God has only the best interests of his children at heart. Women have to be very careful and discerning, not falling prey to cultlike leaders and abusive authority figures who would seek to become "God's voice" for them. God's will, and his call for personal sacrifice—the "at any price" depth of relationship—must be measured against Scripture and tested with good sense.

Women of strength are women of commitment and faithfulness.

How many hot afternoons did Anna spend in the dusty, stifling atmosphere of the temple, waiting for the promised Messiah to appear? In our present day, with everything microwave instant and prepackaged for ease and immediacy, we have very little experience or understanding of this kind of waiting. Putting myself into that picture, I'm sure that after five days, or five weeks, I would have been tempted to say, "I've got better things to do with my time, Lord, than just waiting here for sixty or so years. I've prophesied your appearance until I'm blue in the face—let me know when you're about to make this happen. You know where to find me."

But if we're ever to develop the characteristics of women of strength, to stand firm with a faith tested over time, it is certain that we must learn the value of being women committed to our prayers and faithful to our calling. As a Christian mom, I pray for my children and grandchildren. As a woman of strength, I'll keep doing so until I see those prayers answered—no matter how long it takes.

Women of strength are proven trustworthy.

Can you imagine the eye contact between Paul and Phoebe when he placed his letter to the Roman Christians in her hands? Was there even a word exchanged? Did Paul at that moment need to remind this trustworthy woman he was depending on her? I think not. To even be considered as the courier, evidently Phoebe had already proven her trustworthiness. And how does one do that? It is in smaller issues and responsibilities that our trustworthiness is refined and tested. It is in proving faithful in confidentiality. It is in being faithful in our faith.

We must choose to see even little tasks, incidental conversations, and simple assignments as an opportunity to grow in trustworthiness. I have as my goal to be a woman of strength. I accept the challenge to be trustworthy.

Women of strength aren't afraid to do humble tasks.

Rizpah was known for handling the dead with respect and care. She brought dignity to a task few would have wanted. Let's be women who look for opportunities to do the same. Let's let it affect the very core of our motivation. Isn't that what a woman of strength would do? We know it is.

Women of strength are openhearted, openhanded women.

Both the widow of Zarephath and Dorcas kept open, giving, and serving hearts. No doubt there were those who took advantage of them. Yet, a deep inner compassion can be much stronger than our first impulse of self-preservation. If you and I are ever to learn to be women of strength, we'll look for places to give and to serve—with open hearts and open hands. We will be women who have let the Lord fill us with tenderness and compassion; we will be women who have taken the time and the effort in prayer to prepare ourselves for a selfless, giving life.

Women of strength are gracious.

Those most undeserving are often the very ones God uses to help us learn and develop the strength of graciousness. Certainly people must have abused and taken for granted Martha's gracious gift of hospitality. In fact, didn't we see her in a moment of testing when she turned to Jesus and complained that Mary wasn't helping?[2]

If you and I ever think we're not going to be tested, or that we'll never respond in inappropriate ways as we *grow* into women of strength, we're deceiving ourselves and setting ourselves up for discouragement and failure. Testing, and yes, even failure, are precisely the ways we learn some of our most valuable lessons.

Women of strength are goal-oriented in spiritual things.

As we look at all of the women of strength listed, one thing stands out: They provide living portraits of the inner desire to live as an expression of something deeper, something more than on-the-surface women. Today we would identify this characteristic as the desire to live and be like Christ—to be an accurate representation of Jesus in our relationships, responsibilities, and in our hearts.

These mighty women of strength left us a legacy—a rich heritage of humility, trust, purity, faith, simplicity, self-control, sacrifice, obedience, love of God, and tenacity. A legacy for you and I to pick up and claim for ourselves, and then to pass on to other women. They have shown us by their exemplary lives what it's like to be a real woman—a woman of strength.

Unfortunately, knowing what we ought to be isn't the same as knowing *how* to be what we can be, is it? If we're ever to grow on with our lives, to get from where we are to where we want to be, how to get there is essential.

Are you ready to take those next steps toward being what God has predetermined you can become? The promise of Ephesians 2:10 waits to be our personal experience:

For we are God's workmanship, created in Christ Jesus to do good works, which God prepared in advance for us to do.

It's time. Time that you and I step into our full potential in Christ. To become what he is calling us to be. What a wonderful future lies ahead, planned and prepared in advance by our loving and faithful Almighty God!

✓ Checkpoint:

Make a list of some of your inner characteristics that dissatisfy you.

Which of the characteristics of a *woman of strength* are already in place in your life?

In which of the characteristics do you see needed growth?

Describe your desire to grow into a *woman of strength*.

Can you see any dangers or snares that could lie ahead in your growth?

6

Avoid Driving into the Strong-Woman Quicksand

Before we begin or even continue planning our trip from *here* ✖, growing toward *there* ✖, I must warn you: there is danger lurking right around each and every corner. This trap can insidiously, even silently spring, trapping you in such subtle ways you won't even know you're caught until it's almost too late. A snare has been laid for you as it has for me—a snare that we must go around, circumvent, and avoid.

If I could describe this snare, I would use the definition of a pitfall: a lightly covered, camouflaged pit just waiting to trap us. We can plunge into it easily because we come upon it unexpectedly. Its danger comes unannounced and is promoted by slight shades of error in our thinking and our attitudes.

If unheeded, this snare entangles the most dedicated woman. It enmeshes the committed wife and mother. It hoodwinks young and older women alike. It bamboozles and misleads the spiritually hungry, ensnares the emotionally dry, and even captivates the biblically literate.

This snare is very much like quicksand. Once you step onto

quicksand's deceptive surface it can pull you in, engulfing you without your even knowing where and how it all began.

And once you're caught, you find your course altered toward the pathway of becoming not a woman of strength, but a strong woman. It's true. This awful, deceptive, and dangerous snare can turn you away from becoming the woman of strength you desire to be, and set you up to become a strong woman instead.

Examples of the Strong Woman

Lisa was one such woman. Having been abused by her father, she married early to get away from her dysfunctional situation. However, her husband Harry turned out to be even more abusive than her father. Unsuspecting, Lisa chose a man who fit a certain "emotional" profile and unwittingly perpetuated the very issues in her life she meant to escape. Eventually, Lisa had a string of unsuccessful relationships behind her.

When Lisa finally turned to God, she found a new relationship in Jesus Christ, and as a result, discovered new personal value and worth. She decided to turn her back on her past and to press on. However, in her efforts to be an overcomer, she fell into a much more devastating trap. Without realizing it, Lisa became stronger and stronger. As she gained spiritual knowledge, she also gained an upper-hand attitude. She didn't see it happening. It was subtle at first. She became much less vulnerable to those who had hurt her in the past, and without knowing any better she almost became an untouchable, tough woman. She determined no one would ever hurt her in the same way again. By her own determination to rise above her past, she changed not for the best. Sadly, she became a *strong* woman. The very experiences that could have worked in her to make her tender made her tough and calloused to the needs of others. Eventually she found little tolerance for what she called "victims." She had, after all, found her way out; so why couldn't they?

Elsa did much the same thing. Though she was raised in a Christian home, her father was a strong, domineering figure. She married a very nice Christian man who didn't have quite the same leadership qualities or drive as her father. Then Elsa found that she had leadership capabilities of her own. So she carried on the "family tradition" of holding several key positions in the church. Her husband, however, quietly faded into the background, content to let his wife fulfill church leadership roles and even take spiritual leadership responsibilities in their home. Without even realizing it, Elsa had fallen into the *strong* woman pitfall.

Sela, on the other hand, set out to be a *strong* woman. Raised with older brothers, she learned "how to take care of herself" long before she ever went to school at the age of five. Competitive by nature, Sela felt she had to come out on top in every relational struggle and have the last word in every disagreement. She dominated every Bible study group she attended, and was usually appointed chairman of every committee she joined. Her biblical insight was questionable, but her strong personality kept most people who disagreed with her at bay. Teamwork? Sela would have insisted she was a good team player. But ask those who tried to work with her and they'll tell you it only worked well when she called the shots and everyone else went along with her plan.

The women I have described are obvious examples of *strong* women—strong in personality, motivation, and in obvious personal agenda. But are they the only ones who fall into the strong-woman quicksand? Not on your life. Take Aleshia, for example.

Aleshia is much more complicated and covert. She might even strike you at first meeting as dependable, solid as a rock, and responsible. That's the moment when you realize that counting on her comes with a cost. Her solid-as-a-rock character is really nothing more than cleverly masqueraded rigidity and stiffness. Her welcome has really been enticement and her goal is not co-operation, but control. Does Aleshia ever raise her voice? Probably not, she doesn't have to. In fact, the quieter she gets, the more control she has.

The point I'm making here is simply this: *strong* women don't fit into only one personality category. They aren't all loud, pushy, and offensive. Some are quiet, clever, and manipulative. Not all are easy to spot. Some are quite difficult to identify—difficult because the *strong-ness* I'm referring to here is inward. It's a "heart condi-tion," not a personality disorder.

And, sometimes it's cultural. The differences vary widely in our country between the way people talk to each other and what's acceptable in polite conversation. Raised in super friendly, almost syrupy-sweet Southern California, I had a hard time adjusting to the reserved manners and customs of the Midwest. As my ministry has taken me to every corner of our nation, I have discovered *strong* women who are brash and brassy while other strong women are genteel and charming. The same is true of women of strength. My conclusion is that women of strength cannot be determined or defined by cultural behaviors and styles, neither can strong women be so identified.

So what is it then that makes the difference between strong women and women of strength? The answer lies beyond personality. It transcends culture. The difference is in the heart.

The Woman Within

Since being either a woman of strength or a strong woman is an interior matter, it is necessary to look within. Think about it, are all the smothering or controlling women you know *other* women? If we are honest with ourselves, we will all have to admit that given the right set of circumstances, with just the right cast of characters, the strong woman within us rises without warning.

How about when we're worn out, overextended, and emotionally battered? For me, this is when the strong woman in me wants to come out fighting. My survival instincts merge with my administrative skills and if I'm not careful, I can become harsh and bossy. Yet is this what I really want to be? What about you?

It is the strong woman who is abrasively opinionated, and who pushes her philosophy and "correct" ways on others. It is the woman of strength who can offer alternative suggestions when appropriate, back off when the right to make the decision belongs to another and "pray-wait" it out. Trusting God through a difficult situation gives us strength and takes the "stinger" out of our strong style. Believing in God's grace gives us back our graciousness. Choosing to wait upon God gives us back patience.

Some Friends Discuss Differences Between the Strong Woman and the Woman of Strength

When I asked Christian women about the strong woman definition, many of them responded similarly. Most of them agreed that strong women operate from a position of intimidation, of power, and of manipulation, even if subtle and covert. Several commented on the vast amount of emotional and mental work it took to maintain such strong control and position.

In contrast, they observed that women of strength were more apt to be women of influence, rather than control and that their strength of influence came from the combined credibility of lifestyle, experiences, and inner character, rather than power of position. I listened as women discussed, and determined that the most desirable characteristics of women of strength were their humility, their awareness of their own growth and needs, and their willingness to let God work in them even through difficult situations.

In my discussion groups I heard women define the strong woman as "self-confident" and the woman of strength as "Christ-confident." They commented that while a strong woman appears to have a need to be "the driver," the woman of strength is content to let her life be God-driven. Comments were made that a strong woman must survive—at all costs. That a strong woman will do everything in her power to maintain a "look-good" position in conflict or disagreement. But that, on the contrary, women of strength are willing to let God be their defender and leave their reputation in his care.

The women I questioned also said that the women of strength they knew seem to be content to have only God know the true motivation of their hearts, even when others may misunderstand or criticize their actions or question their motives. In other words, women of strength seem to have overcome the need to be defensive.

Someone mentioned that a strong woman will defend herself to the death. And that while a woman of strength will often remove herself from a conflict, giving God room to resolve it, a strong woman will "stay in there" fighting, quarreling, and shoving her opinions and views until she has badgered her audience or targeted person into admitting defeat or submission.

Other attributes the women in my study groups laid at the feet of the strong-woman type included: she burns out quickly; she moves in the realm of the flesh; she is externally motivated; she is prideful. In contrast, qualities attributed to the woman of strength were: she is internally motivated; she is humble; she has a yielded heart.

In an over-coffee discussion, one woman observed that strong women seem only interested in results and destinations while women of strength take more interest and pay more attention to the details of the journey and their inner personal development along the way. Another woman said that she thought a strong woman lives in the here and now while the woman of strength lives in the *process* of the here and now and how it fits into "later."

Jenny reflected on a particular strong woman in her life and observed that she seems to have "everything figured out" and can handle anything. Yet a woman she saw as a woman of strength readily admits she doesn't have all the answers. She went on to comment, "A woman of strength I know is confident in spite of her weakness. More than once I've watched her draw on the Lord's strength when she had none of her own.

"Come to think of it," Jenny continued, "the woman in my life I consider a *strong woman* has glaring weaknesses she can't even admit. But the *woman of strength's* weaknesses seem insignificant by comparison."

"The strong woman in my life," commented Jan, "flies off the handle and plunges into turmoil when things are beyond her control. She can't leave anything alone until she has forced a show-down. And," she added thoughtfully, "usually not without emotional bloodshed."

"On the other hand," Jackie joined in, "I know someone who is a *woman of strength* who carries peace and confidence with her in the midst of her problems."

"I'd rather be like that," said Mary Ann. She had been quiet throughout our discussion. Now she finally spoke up. "But I have such a long way to go."

"Me too," I agreed.

The room grew quiet. Mary Ann swirled a bit of cold coffee around in her cup. After a while she asked the question foremost on all of our minds. "So, how do we get there?"

We all stared at each other. "It's a big question, isn't it?" I asked, then turned to Mary Ann. "Any ideas?"

"I think," she said softly, "that we get there the same way Jesus did." Slowly she opened her Bible and we waited until she found the verse. "'During the days of Jesus' life on earth, he offered up prayers and petitions with loud cries and tears to the one who could save him from death, and he was heard because of his reverent submission. Although he was a son, he learned obedience from what he suffered … '" (Heb 5:7-8).

"I was afraid of that," Jenny said. Her comment broke the silence and put everyone more at ease.

"That's what it takes, isn't it?" Jan's voice was subdued, thoughtful. "I'm not completely a woman of strength yet," she said, "but I can remember when I was going through a very rough time. I prayed for the situation to change. It didn't. In fact, it seemed only to get worse. Finally, I gave it all to God and then prayed that the situation might change me. No one knew about that prayer except God and me. Being together and talking about this gives me a new understanding of what was going on inside me then."

"Did the situation change you?" Jenny's eyes were wide as she looked at her friend with new insight.

"You bet it did," Jan said. "And as painful as it was—and don't get me wrong, I never want to go through anything like that again—I can honestly say I'm glad it happened." No one pressed her for the details. We all knew what it was to go through a painful experience. We could identify, even sympathize with her. What's more, we could all rejoice with her. Jan didn't fight back the tear that found its way down her cheek. "What happened to me shouldn't happen to anyone. I couldn't reconcile the situation in the light of God's love and care. But over time I have been able to see," she said, staring at the cold, dark liquid in her cup, "that even though it doesn't make sense, with God's help I can make sense out of it. I can finally say that what could have destroyed me has actually given me strength. I can't explain it ... " her voice trailed off.

"I can," Mary Ann said. "It's Romans 8:28 in real life. He's working for our good in all things."

"What exactly do you think changed in you because of what you went through?" I asked.

"Self-righteousness, self-confidence, pride, for starters," Jan said. Then taking a deep breath she told her story. "I was raped. Before that I thought that most girls who were raped brought it on themselves. I knew how to take care of myself—you know, stay away from dark alleys in the wrong part of town, don't wear provocative clothing, don't give wrong signals—I never thought this could happen to me. I had very little compassion for victims of violence before this. That's all changed. I became involved in a rape victim's support system and started a ministry to rape and violence victims in my church. I would have never done that before. I wouldn't have seen the need, nor would I have had the strength."

"See?" Mary Ann said gesturing in Jan's direction. "What did I say? She's Romans 8:28 in person."

"I'm wondering," I said, turning my attention to the entire group. "Could Jan have become a *strong woman* because of this situation?"

"Oh, yes!" Jan was the first to speak up. "At first I was totally devastated and hurt. I had every right. I had been violated! Then I got angry. Angry at those around me for not understanding how hurt I was. Angry at those who had attitudes about rape just like I had before it happened to me. Angry at the perpetrator. Angry at the legal system. Angry at the church for not taking better care of me. Angry at the pastor because he didn't know how it felt to be raped. Angry at the people who wanted me to just put it behind me and get on with my life. Angry at God. I used that anger. It made me feel strong.

"Eventually I realized that my anger wasn't helping—in fact it was hurting me. Friends began backing away. Family members stopped calling. All the while I thought I was being avoided because I had been raped. Only when I took it out on God, in a very strong fit of anger and unchecked emotional prayer, did I see that it wasn't the rape, but what I was letting the fact of the rape do to me. That's where the real danger of damage was. That's when I asked God to let the situation change me. I couldn't change the fact of what happened, but I could change the outcome. It's been more than two years since it happened. I'm a much different person now."

"Different?" I asked. I wanted her to keep talking as long as she would.

"I'm more confident in God's faithfulness. I'm not as fragile as I thought. I can honestly say I'm happier today than I've ever been in my whole life. Out of my deepest pain God has given me purpose. I know he didn't plan for any of this to happen to me. That was the devil's doing. But God took what the devil dished out and by working deep within me, has shoved it all back in the devil's face—and more. I've led several women to Christ through my ministry. Women I would have never been able to reach otherwise."

Is Jan so different? As that thought ran through my mind, I remembered my friend Linda, who lost a child in an accident. I thought of Jeanie—her father was an upstanding leader in the community, but behind closed doors he was a rage-filled alcoholic who beat his wife and kids. And, I thought of Cicily—her husband lost his job and plunged into depression, shifting unmeasurable, never-ending responsibility to her shoulders. Nanette lives with a crippling disease. Elizabeth faces life alone after her husband's suicide. These were women of strength, each one. They prayed the same prayer Jan did—*Lord, change me through this situation.* These women successfully avoided the strong woman pitfall with one simple prayer: *Lord, grow me through this.*

I want to be like them, don't you? I want to be that woman who has the courage to pray for God to change me—not just the situation, but me. If that is also your prayer then let our assurance be the promise of Psalm 91:

He who dwells in the shelter of the Most High will rest in the shadow of the Almighty.

I will say of the LORD, "He is my refuge and my fortress, my God, in whom I trust."

Surely he will save you from the fowler's snare and from the deadly pestilence.

He will cover you with his feathers, and under his wings you will find refuge; his faithfulness will be your shield and rampart.

You will not fear the terror of night, nor the arrow that flies by day, nor the pestilence that stalks in the darkness, nor the plague that destroys at midday.

A thousand may fall at your side, ten thousand at your right hand, but it will not come near you.

You will only observe with your eyes and see the punishment of the wicked.

If you make the Most High your dwelling—even the LORD, who is my refuge—then no harm will befall you, no disaster will come near your tent.

For he will command his angels concerning you to guard you in all your ways; they will lift you up in their hands, so that you will not strike your foot against a stone.

You will tread upon the lion and the cobra; you will trample the great lion and the serpent.

"Because he loves me," says the LORD, "I will rescue him; I will protect him, for he acknowledges my name.

He will call upon me, and I will answer him; I will be with him in trouble, I will deliver him and honor him.

With long life will I satisfy him and show him my salvation.

With our feet headed down a sure pathway, avoiding the pitfall of stepping into the quicksand trap of becoming a *strong woman*— we can continue to progress toward our goal of becoming women of strength. We're not only headed in the right direction, we'll be there sooner than you think.

✓ Checkpoint:

What circumstances in your life can set you up for the pitfall of becoming a *strong woman*?

How can those circumstances help you become a *woman of strength* instead?

What will make the difference?

7

Rebekah—A Strong Woman

It was a day that started like any other; it was, however, a day that would change a young girl's life—forever.[1]

As usual, Rebekah went with the other women of the village down to the spring, filled her jar, and came up again. Leaving the spring, she spotted in the distance a stranger coming toward her. She waited as he approached with his camels and men.

Hurrying to meet her he said, "Please give me a little water from your jar."

"Drink, my lord," she said, and quickly lowered the jar to her hands and gave him a drink. After he had drunk, she said, "I'll draw water for your camels, too, until they have finished drinking." So she quickly emptied her jar into the trough, ran back to the well to draw more water, and drew enough for all his camels.

Without saying a word, the man observed her closely. Rebekah watched him from the corner of her eye. When the camels had finished drinking, the man took a gold nose ring and two gold bracelets from his pouch and gave them to Rebekah. Finally he spoke. "Whose daughter are you? Please tell me, is there room in your father's house for my caravan to spend the night?"

"I am the daughter of Bethuel, the son that Milcah bore to

Nahor," she said. Then she added, "We have plenty of straw and fodder, as well as room for you to spend the night."

She watched in surprise as the man bowed down and worshiped the Lord. "Praise be to the Lord," he said. "The Lord, the God of my master Abraham, has not abandoned his kindness and faithfulness to my master." Then he said to Rebekah, "As for me, the Lord has led me on the journey to the house of my master's relatives."

Turning, she ran toward her mother's house. As quickly as she could, she told the entire household about the man and displayed the fine jewelry he had given her.

Curious, Rebekah's brother Laban went to meet the generous man. Who was he? What did he want? As soon as he had seen the nose ring, and the bracelets on his sister's arms, and had heard Rebekah tell what the man said to her, he knew this was no ordinary event, no ordinary visitor. He found the stranger still standing by the camels near the spring.

"Come, you who are blessed by the Lord," he said. "Why are you standing out here? I have prepared the house and a place for the camels."

So they went to the house, and the camels were unloaded. Straw and fodder were brought for them, and water for the visitor and his men to wash their feet. Then food was set before him, but he said, "I will not eat until I have told you what I have to say."

"Then tell us," Laban said.

"I am Abraham's servant," the humble man explained. "The Lord has blessed my master abundantly, and he has become wealthy. He has given him sheep and cattle, silver and gold, menservants and maidservants, and camels and donkeys." He paused and Laban saw the weariness of the man's trip wash over him.

"Eat," he said, "then tell us the rest. Refresh yourself first."

"No," the man said. "I must continue. My master's wife, Sarah, has borne him a son in her old age, and my master has given his son everything he owns. My master made me swear an oath, and said, 'You must not get a wife for my son from the daughters of the Canaanites, in whose land I live, but go to my father's family and to my own clan, and get a wife for my son.'"

"I see," Laban said. He had guessed right; this was no ordinary visitor, nor was this an ordinary visit. *Get to the point*, Laban demanded inwardly.

"Then I asked my master," the man went on, "'What if the woman will not come back with me?' My master replied, 'The Lord, before whom I have walked, will send his angel with you and make your journey a success, so that you can get a wife for my son from my own clan and from my father's family. Then, when you go to my clan, you will be released from your oath even if they refuse to give her to you.'" The visitor wiped his forearm across his forehead.

"When I came to the spring today, I said, 'O Lord, God of my master Abraham, if you will, please grant success to the journey on which I have come. See, I am standing beside this spring; if a maiden comes out to draw water and I say to her, "Please let me drink a little water from your jar," and if she says to me, "Drink, and I'll draw water for your camels too," let her be the one the Lord has chosen for my master's son.'"

"And?" Laban said as his heart beat faster. "Go on," he urged, even though he guessed what the man would say next.

"Before I finished praying in my heart, Rebekah came out with her jar on her shoulder. She went down to the spring and drew water, and I said to her, 'Please give me a drink.' She quickly lowered her jar from her shoulder and said, 'Drink, and I'll water your camels, too.' So I drank, and she watered the camels."

"I see." Laban felt as though God himself was speaking to him about his sister.

"I asked her, 'Whose daughter are you?' She said, 'The daughter of Bethuel son of Nahor, whom Milcah bore to him.' Then I put the ring in her nose and the bracelets on her arms, and I bowed down and worshiped the Lord. I praised the Lord, the God of my master Abraham, who had led me on the right road to get the granddaughter of my master's brother for his son. Now if you will show kindness and faithfulness to my master, tell me; and if not, tell me, so I may know which way to turn." And as he said this, Laban could see the urgency in his eyes.

Laban and Bethuel conferred, then Laban answered for them both, "This is from the Lord; we can say nothing to you one way or the other. Here is Rebekah; take her and go, and let her become the wife of your master's son, as the Lord has directed."

When Abraham's servant heard what they said, he bowed down to the ground before the Lord.

Then the servant brought out gold and silver jewelry and articles of clothing and gave them to Rebekah; he also gave costly gifts to her brother and to her mother. Then he and the men who were with him ate and drank and spent the night there. When they got up the next morning, he said, "Send me on my way to my master."

But her brother and her mother replied, "Let the girl remain with us ten days or so; then you may go."

"Oh, no," the servant of Abraham said, "Do not detain me, now that the Lord has granted success to my journey. Send me on my way so I may go to my master."

"Let's call the girl and ask her about it," they said. "Will you go with this man?" they asked when she responded to their call.

"I will go," she said.

It was settled. She would go to Abraham's son, Isaac, and become his wife. But she was also to be so much more. For you see, even though she didn't know it at the time, Rebekah was also on her way to becoming a strong woman. Though a focal character in one of the most romantic stories in all the Bible, Rebekah was about to change. She was to become a woman who, little by little, began to take things, circumstances, and people into her own hands to manipulate them to her own ends for her own purposes. It didn't happen all at once. It took many years.

For twenty years, Rebekah was the love of Isaac's life. He doted on this woman twenty years his junior. When he was nearly sixty, Isaac petitioned the Lord on her behalf, because she was barren.

Soon the Lord answered Isaac's prayer and Rebekah became pregnant. Nearly forty, and in her first pregnancy, she was miserable. Twin babies jostled each other within her. "Why is this happening to me?" she cried out to the Lord.

The Lord spoke to her and said, "Two nations are in your womb, and two peoples from within you will be separated; one people will be stronger than the other, and the older will serve the younger."

When the time came, she gave birth to twins. The first to come out was red, and his whole body was like a hairy garment; so they named him Esau (which means "red"). After this, his brother came out, with his hand grasping Esau's heel; so he was named Jacob (which means "supplanter").

And so it began, Rebekah's journey to becoming a strong woman. Based on a word from the Lord, she chose to favor the child she thought the Lord favored. She openly preferred Jacob over Esau. Isaac, perhaps in reaction to his wife's open favoritism, doted on Esau, and a split in the family between husband and wife began. Rebekah stood at a moment of choice and instead of letting the Lord work out what he had told her, she took matters into her own hands to make sure it happened. No matter who got hurt, no matter what the cost to her husband and her other son, Jacob would have the rights and privileges belonging to his brother. The Lord said it, and Rebekah would make it happen.

Just as it might happen with women like you and me, Rebekah changed from being a hardworking, industrious woman of faith into a manipulative deceiver. What a change from the simplicity of a trusting young girl at Laban's well to this! The mother of such opposite twins developed a dark side. A household of love turned into a household of jealousy and strife.

Rebekah's story has a sad ending. While Esau was the one who stayed near home, he married wives who drove Rebekah crazy. He saw no reason to even try to please her. Jacob, her favorite son, was forced to flee for his life. Her deceptive manipulation drove away from her side the very son she preferred. There is no indication that she ever saw Jacob's children and had the joy of being their grandmother.

The hard lesson learned is this: strong women often drive away or lose those very people they try so hard to control. A woman who sought to use God and his plan to serve her own interests, Rebekah reveals deep inner character weakness. She was indeed a classic *strong woman.*

Think about it, have you ever been tempted to use God, or anyone else for that matter, to serve your own interests? I ask myself the same question. If I were to be perfectly honest, I'd have to admit I'm not always happy with the answers. How about you?

But I have good news. We don't have to stay caught in the "Rebekah trap" any longer. The trap of manipulation and deceit is not for women of strength. There is a better way. As we saw in previous chapters, other women in the Bible and even some of our most respected contemporary women show us a different, better way to be, grow, and live. We don't have to be *Rebekahs,* we can grow into *Abigails.*

✓ Checkpoint:

How do the lessons of Rebekah relate to the definitive *strong woman* you identified at the end of the introductory chapter?

If you think about it, have you ever been tempted to use God, or anyone else, to serve your own interests? Be specific.

Can you identify one or more Rebekah traps you feel caught in now? Comment.

Are you interested in changing? Why or why not?

8

The Life and Times of
a Woman of Strength

To become a woman of strength, I must have as my life's goals:

To live and be like Christ.

To live guileless, full of faith, and obedient to his will.

To hold to simplicity in my walk with him, guarding my heart against duplicity.

To know God's will and pursue it.

To be willing to submit to whatever it takes to develop his characteristics within me.

Ouch! Do I really mean *whatever* it takes? I most certainly do.

Identifying Women of Strength

As I said in chapter six, there are several characteristics that we can draw from women we see as women of strength. But there is more. Drawing on the examples of the women we have already looked at previously, let's learn how to identify the women of strength that live right around us. My prayer is that you first learn to draw your own conclusions from your study of biblical women. Then learn from the lives of your own personal heroines and living, breathing women of strength. Begin to identify women of strength by certain common threads that run through their lives.

Women of strength open their deepest inner selves to God, without reservation, regardless of their past or pain.

We've seen this over and over in the lives of the women we've mentioned so far. But I'm convinced that within arm's reach of each of us there are women of strength—women who are completely open to God; who hold nothing back from him, who have dreadful pain in their pasts; but who have been made sweet, not bitter by it. Open your eyes to such women who may be living within touching distance—physically, emotionally, and spiritually. A woman of strength may be closer than you think.

Women of strength seem to have an inner handle on God's will.

One of the most remarkable things I look for when identifying women of strength is that they have settled, deep within their hearts, the issue of God's will. Every decision they make seems to submit to it. They know why they do what they do, in light of their relationship to God through Jesus Christ. When these women do what they don't want to do (They are still human you know, just like you and me!), they unhesitatingly point to some issue or area not yet surrendered to God's will. Then they pray until they know what needs to be done.

Women of strength have a passion for God's call on their lives.

My friend Carol's ministry to the deaf has required that those of us who love her release her to follow the passionate and distinct purpose God has for her life. She has sacrificially but willingly abandoned the hearing world, to enter a complete culture of its own—the world of the deaf. Miss her as I may, I cannot allow my friendship to hold her back; there is a much higher calling on her life than being an always-in-touch friend to me. Carol is a woman of strength.

Without a doubt, God's call on my life is ministry through writing. I've made many adjustments to accommodate my call. I've learned to live with solitude, sometimes even silence, to think and pray alone. Writing isn't done in a group. It's done alone. My friends have had to adjust to my need for solitude. My church activities have to be woven around my calling. My family has made adjustments. Do I love the work? Not always. It's hard work, physically, mentally, and spiritually. Do I love my calling? *Passionately!*

Claudia sensed the call of God on her life concerning children. Not healthy, whole kids, but kids nobody wanted or needed. Kids with problem histories of abuse, neglect, and molestation. Is her mission always fun? It's rarely fun and seldom rewarding. Does she love it? Not always. Is she passionate about her calling? *Indeed.* Claudia is a woman of strength.

Look around. When you find a woman with a passion for God's call on her life you will find a woman of strength.

Women of strength have an ability to illuminate the way for others through scriptural principles and sound doctrine, no matter what contemporary culture may say or which current of doctrinal breeze may be blowing.

I dedicated this book to a special friend and mentor, Barbara

Tollefson. She is an illuminator. Never dogmatic in insisting I do what she says or believe exactly the way she does, she nearly hand-fed me for eight years. She fed me spiritually and emotionally with her love for me. She loved me just as I was. She also nourished me through her unwavering commitment to Christ, her love for God's Word, and her probing questions that often sent me scurrying for answers and insight. She was a carrot dangler, encouraging me to go just a little farther, to move in just a little deeper, and to press on just a bit harder. She taught me to pray and to trust and to have faith in what God was doing in me and what he will do in me still.

Once in a while, though nearly eighteen years have passed and we are two thousand miles apart, I still long to go to her house, sit with a cup of coffee and ask, "What's the Lord doing in you lately?" then unhurriedly sip my coffee and just listen. Open and transparent with her own life and heart before the Lord, this woman of strength shows me the way of submission, humility, and true servanthood. Barbara lights the pathway, not only for me, but for countless others. She is a woman of strength. I pray that God gives *you* someone just like her.

Women of strength aren't afraid to touch the untouchable.

Look around. Do you see special women who touch the untouchable? Women who appear with just the right action or word when no one else seems to know what to do or say? Women who aren't afraid to touch a dying person? To talk to unkempt strangers at church? Or who spend themselves for the lonely? Women who care for the elderly? Or who will hold a dirty drug addict? Women who volunteer for hospice service? Or who minister to AIDS-infected people or crack-affected babies? When you do, remind yourself, "I'm in the company of a woman of strength."

Women of strength have a practical, down-to-earth approach in their prayer lives.

A woman of strength never, never needs to speak in anything other than friendly—even intimate—terms with God. Because God has already met her at her level of communication and need, she has no desire to impress you, me, or anybody with the "spirituality" of her prayers. When you find such a woman, hang on. Let her teach you to pray.

Women of strength seem to exude practical applications for deeply spiritual insights.

My friend Barb once asked me how I was doing. "I'm really under it," I moaned.

"You are?" she asked with surprise. "But, the Bible says we are seated in heavenly places with Christ Jesus. Maybe you're looking at this from the wrong side."

In a neighborhood Bible study one day, another young woman complained that her husband wasn't as close to the Lord as she would like him to be.

"Maybe," Barb explained softly, "you could just hold him up in prayer more. If you did that, he'd at least be as close to God as you can reach."

Another time, Barb asked, "If God were to deal with your husband, could you stay out of his way?" These are insights of a woman of strength.

Women of strength are encouragers—not controllers.

It seems that women of strength have no need or hidden agendas to force their methods, ideas, or standards on those they mentor or mother. They do, however, have a way of encouraging those "under their care" toward being better, stronger, deeper Christians.

Such women possess the rare quality of stubborn love—love that isn't easily moved or shaken, but that hangs tough for all their spiritual "children." Love that encourages and challenges growth.

*   *   *

Though I'd like to say I'm an accomplished woman in all of these areas, I'm not. I am, however, still growing toward them. How about you? Are you there yet? Can you say that in your love of God, in service, sacrifice, and devotion to Christ you have it completely in hand? If you are like me and see growth in one area of your life and the need for growth in others, take heart. We can grow *there* ✖ from *here* ✖. Want more compassion? Want stronger commitment and ability to persevere? Need stronger faith? Firmer trust in God? To be more committed to his agenda and purposes rather than your own? Me too.

I want to sow good seeds, seeds of strength, not only in my own life, but in the lives of my daughters and granddaughters, and in the lives of those who look to me for mentoring. I want to leave a legacy worth carrying to those who will come after me. The prayer of my heart is to be a woman of strength, fully alive, full of purpose and mission. I want to be like Christ. How about you? Are we together in this?

If we are serious about becoming more like Christ and

becoming women of strength, it is a good idea to write this goal down somewhere. Knowing that we stand *here*, it's time we identified more specifically *where* we want to grow from here. The next chapter will help you draft a life's mission (purpose) statement, to give you a clear cut picture of exactly where *there* is for you. Just keep this one thing in mind, no matter where you are now, you *can* get there from here.

✓ Checkpoint:

How are you more willing to open your deepest inner self to God, without reservation, regardless of your past or pain than you were when you first started reading this book?

What part of your past or personal pain is still difficult to open to God?

Do you have an "inner handle" on God's will? Explain.

What characteristics common to women of strength listed in this chapter do you see evident in your life?

Which of the characteristics do you want to see more of in your life?

How do you think this could happen?

9

Where Exactly, Is There?

A nyone who has ever traveled with children is familiar with the much repeated question, "Are we there yet?" One of my children once added a particularly humorous question, "Where, exactly, is *there*, anyway?" I knew it was time to introduce that child to the wonderful world of maps. Old enough to read the freeway signs, she was delighted with charting our course. Then, when either of the other two asked the question, "Are we there yet?" she was eager to respond. "No," she'd say with confidence, "we're only halfway there. We have to go through (whatever city or town was next on the map), first."

Getting to *there* is much like discovering the world of maps and charts. Not only do we need to know where we are going, but also where we've been, what we've come through as well as milestones and landmarks yet ahead. A personal mission statement is an effective tool that will bring our destination into clear focus. Once we have that clearly defined, our charted course becomes more evident.

We usually think of mission statements in terms of corporations, organizations, and ministries. Even inner departments of big organizations must operate with a clearly focused mission statement in keeping with a bigger, overall mission statement of the parent company. It's much the same for us. If we are to become women of strength, it is because we do so on purpose, with the guidance and governing help of a personal mission statement.

In the last chapter, I opened with a statement of my goals for becoming a woman of strength. These can be simplified into one sentence: *To become a woman of strength, I choose to have as my life's goal to live and be like Christ.* This statement is simple enough to be remembered, challenging enough to make me stretch. You see, if I am honest with you and with myself, I will admit that while that statement is truly the desire and cry of my heart, I still have a long way to *grow*. Often I am tempted to moan, "How much farther, Lord? Am I there yet?"

Focused Goals of Growth

If I embrace as my personal mission and goal to live and be like Christ, I have to look at his life from the pages of the Bible and pattern not only my mission statement but my very life after what I find present in his life. Then I know what areas of continual growth I can expect. Remember, we don't become women of strength by some supernatural, instantaneous zap of God's Holy Spirit, but by purposely and intently growing into his best for us. We do this by having several focused goals of growth.

To become a woman of strength, I must want to know God's will and be willing to pursue it.

Jesus said, "For I have come down from heaven not to do my will but to do the will of him who sent me" (Jn 6:38). Everything

Jesus did yielded and submitted to that one statement. He had come to do God's will. It was a stated fact, a settled issue. Jesus was here on kingdom business.

You and I are on kingdom business as well. Not citizens of this world,[1] we live here only until God calls us to leave this world and live with him forever. Furthermore, while we are here, we live as ambassadors for him.[2] Not free to do our own will, but freed from our sins to do his. Psalm 40, verse 8 then becomes our deepest prayer: "I desire to do your will, O my God; your law is within my heart." With a focused goal and a heart prayer, we will find areas of opportunity and growth.

To become a woman of strength, I must desire to live a life full of faith.

That's the way Jesus lived. Isaiah prophesied that the Messiah would be without craftiness, manipulation, or trickery when he said, "nor was any deceit in his mouth."[3] Can this be said about me? Do I color the truth when it serves me? Or am I frank, candid, and forthright? Do people really believe what I am saying, or do they search for hidden meaning behind my words? And when caught in a fault, do I defend myself with the fancy footwork of frivolous verbiage, or do I have enough faith to leave my defense up to God? Do you?

To become a woman of strength I will learn to hold to simplicity in my walk with him, to guard my heart against complicatedness and duplicity.

Sometimes it's so tempting to cover, to hide my need for growth by pretending I'm already there. It's so natural to want to look my best. It's easy to resort to sounding spiritually superior, to know the words, but to be personally unfamiliar with their deepest meaning.

Jesus was so simple in his responses. I'm always amazed at how he handled criticism. While never sidestepping, he often deflected his accusers with a simple, but well put, personally poignant question. He never pretended. Do I? Do you? Will I ever get there? Will you?

To become a woman of strength, I will learn to submit to whatever it takes to develop Christlike characteristics.

It is only when I can define my struggles and difficulties with this perspective that I can begin to understand experientially the full personal implications of the words of James in chapter one, verses 2-5:

Consider it pure joy, my brothers, whenever you face trials of many kinds, because you know that the testing of your faith develops perseverance. Perseverance must finish its work so that you may be mature and complete, not lacking anything. If any of you lacks wisdom, he should ask God, who gives generously to all without finding fault, and it will be given to him.

Mature? Complete? A woman of strength. I want to grow there—how about you?

To become a woman of strength, I will learn how to honor God in my thoughts, behavior, relationships, and work.

Colossians 1:18 says, "So that in everything he might have the supremacy." If I want to become a godly woman of strength, it will never do to keep the place of supremacy in my life for myself.

If I am to honor God, he will be the One I honor above myself. I will have to give him the freedom to examine my thoughts and to govern my behavior, and I will glorify him in my relationships and in my work. My cherished goal will be not only integrity, but god-liness.

To become a woman of strength, I will learn to provide encouragement where it is appropriate and needed.

The Sovereign LORD has given me an instructed tongue, to know the word that sustains the weary. He wakens me morning by morning, wakens my ear to listen like one being taught.[4]

The weary are everywhere. People struggling with life need encouragement. It's up to us to reach out to such people with an uplifting word or a deed of hope and help. And I do; sometimes I do too much.

You see, an untaught tongue, even when attempting to give a word of encouragement, can get in God's way of doing what he wants to do in someone else's life. It's true. Only when I seek him for his guidance can I make sure a word or deed meant to encourage is not only needed, but appropriate and in keeping with God's will.

To become a woman of strength, I will learn to see opportunity and know whether it is appropriate to model or to speak God's Word.

Restraint. How easy it is to look into the lives and situations of others and confront, correct, or even attempt to control with a well-aimed Bible passage—a direct "word" from God. But is that always the most effective approach? Remember, women of strength seek to honor God in *everything* they do and say. Using his Word and our "maturity" inappropriately to bring about *our* desired results instead of *his* doesn't line up with his commandment to speak the truth. It is possible to do more damage than good that way.

On the other hand, a woman of strength learns to speak with authority when appropriate. What's the deciding factor? Sensitivity to the leading of the Holy Spirit and making sure nothing of *me* gets in the way.

To become a woman of strength, I must lead others into a personal or deepening relationship with Jesus Christ.

Personally, I'd rather teach or instruct than lead. Come on, am I so different than you? Leading takes patience, it means lovingly and supportively watching others attempt, and even fail. It means involvement. Isn't that what Jesus did in his dealing with the disciples? He taught them, of course, but he also led. He poured himself into twelve unlikely, rough men. He carefully chose his words as he led them into strength and faith to become the early church. What he gave them lasted after his departure—kept them until the Holy Spirit came on the day of Pentecost.

Women of strength do that. I'm living proof. The women of strength who have crossed my pathway have left their strongest impressions on my life through example, commitment, and willingness to lead, not control or manage. Like the Shepherd who leads us all beside the still waters, so many women of strength have taken the time to lead me. And if I am ever to be like Christ, like them, I'll learn to lead as well.

"Are we there yet?" Can you and I honestly say we measure up to the personal mission statement and growth goals outlined above? Is the destination too far to go, impossible to reach? Of course it is—at least without God's help and perhaps one of his women of strength to help us. In the next chapter we'll speak more about that very thing.

But, before we look there, let's give our sample personal mission statement a test. Let's ask some hard questions.

Testing the Personal Mission Statement

1. If a personal mission statement is to stand the test of time and be used for God's purposes in our lives, it must reflect current desire and direction as well as lay the groundwork for growth and change in the years to come. Does our sample do that? It does for me, how about you?

2. When I implement my personal mission statement, will it communicate clearly through my lifestyle, choices, and attitudes that God is at work in me? Does it provide me with a challenging motivation to change and grow?

3. Does this personal mission statement help me identify those things in my life that need improving or have become a distraction or detour from what God wants me to be or do?

4. Can I put this statement to use immediately? Does it help me see where I am, and where I need growth right now?

5. Does this personal mission statement give me hope in the knowledge that other women are *growing* there too?

6. Will this statement serve as a good point of reference when I'm making decisions—seeking direction and wisdom in relation-

ships, areas of responsibility, ministry, or areas of service and involvement?

A personal mission statement such as I have outlined in this chapter can serve each of us well as we open ourselves to God and his purposes for us. It should stay fluid and adaptable in its application to the changing seasons of our lives. When I take the time to revisit my personal mission statement, to review it reflectively and prayerfully, I should experience the changes God intends within me to grow into his woman of strength.

How will we get *there* from *here*? Don't be discouraged. We have just barely identified where *there* really is! Our route has to be carefully planned and thought through. We're growing on purpose, you and I. And with just a few important factors in mind, we *can* grow *there* from *here*.

✓ Checkpoint:

If you were to begin writing your own personal mission statement, what would be a good beginning sentence? Write it down.

What else would you like to include in your personal mission statement? Continue writing. This will be your first draft. When you have finished this first draft, examine it according to the "test" on page eighty-five. Rewrite and revise as necessary.

10

Mentors–Close Encounters of the Strengthening Kind

When I need to travel from my home in central California to a distant or unknown city, I have learned it's best to consult someone with more expertise in dealing with all the necessary details and information. "Where do you want to go?" the travel agent asks. Her fingers poised at the keyboard of her computer terminal, she is ready to type in whatever information I give her and read screens of schedules and data quite unfamiliar to me. "And when?" she asks as she works with more information. Then, "You're coming home when?" I wait. She works for a few minutes, then turns to me with options to consider. I make my choices. Within a few minutes she has me booked on a flight, and I leave her office with my ticket in hand. My trip, my plans, my destination are all made possible and almost hassle-free with her help.

We would do well to engage such a "travel agent" or "trip consultant" as we grow from *here* ✖ to *there* ✖ . We need someone to help us who has expertise, knows the details, understands the possible pitfalls and obstacles that we are apt to encounter as we grow into women of strength.

Travel Agents for Our Journey

I'm talking about finding someone like my friends Barb, Marieta, and Judy—my loving and patient mentors. These are women who have all helped me grow in specific, as well as general, ways. They have helped me more than they will ever know through their friendship and guidance toward becoming the woman of strength I desire to be.

In the Bible, Ruth looked to Naomi for mentoring. Often referred to as the most romantic story in the entire Bible,[1] the account concerns Naomi's guidance and counsel as much as Boaz's romantic interest in Ruth.

Both Naomi and Ruth enjoyed the security of their lifelong commitment to each other, and both tasted the sweet fruit of their personal investment in one another. Ruth married Boaz and placed the baby from that marriage in the arms of Naomi. Ruth got a husband, and Naomi a grandson.

In the New Testament we find another significant mentoring relationship—Mary and Elizabeth's. Pregnant with God's Son and our Savior, Mary needed someone she could talk to. She went to see Elizabeth, her older cousin. Elizabeth carried within her womb the baby who would be John the Baptist, God's announcer of the Messiah. The book of Luke records it beautifully.

Mary got ready and hurried to a town in the hill country of Judea, where she entered Zechariah's home and greeted Elizabeth. When Elizabeth heard Mary's greeting, the baby leaped in her womb, and Elizabeth was filled with the Holy Spirit.

In a loud voice [Elizabeth] exclaimed: "Blessed are you among women, and blessed is the child you will bear! But why am I so favored, that the mother of my Lord should come to me? As soon as the sound of your greeting reached my ears, the baby in my womb leaped for joy. Blessed is she who has believed that what the Lord has said to her will be accomplished!"

And Mary said: "My soul glorifies the Lord and my spirit rejoices in God my Savior, for he has been mindful of the humble state of his servant. From now on all generations will call me blessed, for the Mighty One has done great things for me— holy is his name. His mercy extends to those who fear him, from generation to generation. He has performed mighty deeds with his arm; he has scattered those who are proud in their inmost thoughts. He has brought down rulers from their thrones but has lifted up the humble. He has filled the hungry with good things but has sent the rich away empty. He has helped his servant Israel, remembering to be merciful to Abraham and his descendants forever, even as he said to our fathers."

Mary stayed with Elizabeth for about three months and then returned home.[2]

One can only imagine the conversation shared between these two women during those three months. Each knew the beauty and magnificence of God's miracle growing within them. Both knew the unlikelihood of such events happening in their day, much less in their family! Was Mary ever confused? Probably so, at times. But for three months she had Elizabeth for support. Did she doubt? Maybe. But then Elizabeth's baby had actually leapt within her womb when he heard Mary's voice. I'm confident Elizabeth would have reminded Mary of that wonderful happening whenever she could. Was Mary ever scared? I would be, wouldn't you?

But of course, she had her mentor—Elizabeth.

We need other women in our lives. Not just friendships of women, but deep, helping relationships. Someone to help us, to give support for what God is doing in our hearts and lives. We need someone like Elizabeth. Someone who also knows what it's like when God does something unusual. We need someone older, more experienced, wiser in areas where we are lacking. We each need a mentor.

What Is a Mentor?

Your mentor must have a few essential qualifications if she is to help you grow into a woman of strength. Your mentor must be a godly woman, a growing woman of strength, a woman of integrity, prayer, and support.

Often such mentors are available, but overlooked. Women of strength don't always stick out like other women. They are not always as obvious as the strong women in your circle of acquaintances. They are not as needy as the weak women you know. They won't push their way into your life or affairs. Many times they simply offer their friendship. If you want their help, you'll have to ask for it. You see, women of strength are more than happy to help, but they don't need you to need them. Secure in their relationship with the Lord, they welcome those he puts into their lives. They want only his best purpose for themselves and also for you. Mentoring women of strength wait until you recognize what they discovered for themselves: that women really do need each other. Someone was there for them, and now they are there for you. Look around, you'll see them—probably hugging someone.

A mentor is, of course, a spiritual counselor.

She is someone with whom you can have a mutual exchange of ideas, opinions, discussion, and deliberation; someone who will give you advice after, not before such exchanges and deliberation; someone who will make helpful recommendations, rather than personally motivated demands.

Such a mentor is a patient listener. She is someone who makes a point of listening, and is not just listening while waiting to make her own point. A true mentor is open, willing to be vulnerable enough to risk resistance or even an open challenge to her own opinions. She recognizes that she, too, is still in process, and as strange as it may seem, is willing to learn from you as you learn from her.

A mentor is an advisor with whom you can share perspectives, problems, and struggles without fear of judgment.

She is someone who will listen to ideas and solutions and give advice that assists you toward making your *own* decisions without imposing or requiring that you follow *her* suggestions.

A mentor serves as a guide.

Your mentor should be someone with whom you can openly share your confusion, questions, or perplexing situations, and she will help you see the way for yourself. She is someone who isn't afraid to point out the way, but respects your right to make your own decisions and make your own mistakes; someone who serves as a model in her walk with the Lord; someone who shepherds, not drives others toward actions and solutions.

A mentor is a confidant.

She is one who can be close without stifling or smothering and she can be trusted to be confidential. She is someone to whom you can confide intimate matters or secrets without fear of betrayal.

An effective mentor is a spiritual leader.

She is someone who has walked where you walk, been where you are now, and has successfully navigated the path you see stretched out before you. She knows and understands the discipline of prayer and exemplifies ongoing growth in her own life.

A mentor knows how to be a coach.

She is someone you can look to as an instructor and trainer in matters of inner strength and character. She's one who knows how to be that particular someone you can look to for signals and directions when in doubt or facing a decision.

A mentor is someone you can depend on for personal attention. She is willing to impart her knowledge or skill to help you develop into a woman of strength, willing to let you learn by personal discovery (even when that means making a mistake or asking a dumb question). A mentor believes implicitly in God's plans and purposes for you.

A mentor is also a tutor.

She is one who knows that you need *individual* instruction as God does a unique work within you. She knows you are a designer original and she is more interested in your success in becoming what God wants you to be than in what she wants you to be. She is in the business of discipling Christ's followers, not in cloning herself.

A mentor is a luminary.

A mentor sheds light with scriptural insight, encourages you to learn to recharge your own battery, and also challenges you to become a luminary for others.

A mentor is often an intercessor.

She is someone who prays for you, then shows you how to pray for yourself, and then motivates you to pray for others.

A mentor is your best advocate and will be supportive.

As such, your mentor will encourage you to stand on your own two feet, confident that you will succeed. She will defend you to others, but lovingly confront you when necessary.

And most of all, a mentor is a true friend.

A mentor knows you inside and out, "warts and all," and loves you anyway. She lets you have the freedom to be yourself, respects your "different-ness" and "separate-ness," and encourages you to grow even if that growth takes you away from her.

Where do you find such mentoring friends? They are right around you. You might look within your family or your church. Your Bible study or prayer group may have the mentor that you need.

✓ Checkpoint:

List the names of the women you have looked to in a mentoring relationship in the past.

Have you picked *women of strength* or *strong women?* (Refer to chapter seven if necessary.)

List the names of some of the women you now realize are *women of strength.*

What can you do to encourage relationships with them?

Part Two

The Journey:
Becoming a Woman
of Strength

With the concepts of the previous chapters firmly in your mind, you are on your way to becoming a woman of strength. Your bags are all packed and you are nearly out the door, ready to travel to your destination.

The second part of this book will actually describe the route toward *there*, toward becoming a woman of strength, with points of interest, rest stops, and a little "inner" sightseeing all built into your personal itinerary.

Don't forget your mentor, for she is a special woman God will use to help you avoid the pitfalls and unnecessary detours. She can help you identify roadblocks, barriers, and help you plan alternate courses when necessary.

Okay, here are your directions: Begin at "here." Stop at Quiet Time Square. Be sure to pause frequently at Prayer Pulloff. Turn right at Discipline Drive. Go down Reclamation Road. Proceed through Problem Pass. Take the Desert Crossing. Detour through Death Valley. Stop at Eagle Rock Lookout. Refuel at Powerhouse Point. This route may sound unfamiliar to you, but, believe me, it is a trail "blazed" by the likes of Ruth, Esther, and Mary the mother of Jesus. It's the most direct path to "there." So get ready, let's grow!

11

Quiet Time Square

In the middle of Ligonier, Pennsylvania, sits a little park, encircled by the business center of the small, picturesque city. The neatly landscaped town square with its mature trees and large shrubs has obviously been there a long time. And right in the middle of the beautiful little square is a proud Victorian style gazebo.

Any time of the day, you can see someone making use of the little retreat. A sales clerk takes in the warm sun before her store opens. She sits across from a man feeding the squirrels. Later on in the day you see a young woman taking advantage of the conveniently-located getaway to eat her sack lunch, or a mother and child enjoying an ice cream cone from the store down the street. These are real-life Norman Rockwell scenes.

I picture that gazebo whenever I read the words of Psalms 62:5, "Find rest, O my soul, in God alone; my hope comes from him." For me, the town square in Ligonier is a picture of the inner life of a woman of strength—a woman who knows the value of quietness in the middle of her busy life, a woman who frequents solitude because of who she is in Christ and who Christ is in her.

Stop at Quiet Time Square.

The women of strength I know and love maintain the daily habit of quiet time. Quiet times, devotions, or whatever you may call your practice, is a *place* and *space* we choose to create in our lives so that we can meet with God. In this age of driven and busy people, quiet time is frequently a neglected discipline. But without a devotional practice, daily life becomes shallow and vague. With a vital devotional time, our lives are opened to the privilege and pleasure of God's presence.[1]

I see women of strength making place and space for a personal, devotional relationship with God. They create a little place in the center of their busy and challenging lives. They're not trying to escape or withdraw from life's realities, but to seek solitude, a bit of seclusion, a brief separation from the hubbub of life for a few precious moments. Alone with God.

They have created for themselves the discipline of the daily sabbatical. Henri Nouwen says it like this:

Because our secular milieu offers us so few spiritual disciplines, we have to develop our own. We have, indeed, to fashion our own "desert" where we can withdraw every day, shake off our compulsions, and dwell in the gentle healing presence of our Lord.[2]

A simple refuge, a sanctuary of privacy where we can reconnect regularly with the presence of the Lord. Maybe you don't have a gazebo to sit in. You probably don't have a cottage waiting just for your personal devotional time. But most of us can retreat to a dining room table, or find our devotional haven in the living room recliner or out on the deck. We just need someplace for a bit of quiet with God so that we can tend to interior matters.

Gordon MacDonald says that "he who orders his inner spiritual world will make a place for God to visit and speak. And when that voice is heard, it will be unlike anything else ever spoken."[3]

Let's dwell for a moment on more thoughts from these two wonderful authors.

1. "God wants to become our daily food and drink."

—Henri J. Nouwen[4]

Jesus taught his disciples to pray for their daily bread. In our quiet time we can actually experience his spiritual food nourishing our inner selves, feeding the emerging woman of strength within.

2. "The very first thing we need to do is set apart a time and a place to be with God and him alone."—Henri J. Nouwen

In our busy days, in the middle of family activities and in the rush of our mornings, it's very difficult to get time alone. Yet, Pastor Jack Hayford advises that we find a few moments we can take from the evening before, or move our schedules up so that we get up a little earlier—we can make the time.[5] Thomas H. Green calls this "the remote preparation." Starting the evening before, a biblical passage can be selected and studied—you may even want to search through commentaries to prepare yourself ahead of time for your quiet meditation on God's Word the next morning. "Without this remote preparation," Thomas Green says, "we will not be doing what we can to open ourselves to God. We will be coming to prayer too casually, taking God for granted."[6]

3. "If my private world is in order, it will be because I am unafraid to be alone and quiet before Christ."—Gordon MacDonald

Could one of the reasons we don't create this discipline for ourselves be that we *are* afraid to be alone and quiet before Christ?

Are we afraid of what he might see or say concerning our inner life and the secrets of our hearts? Are we afraid he might address our motives? Lately, I've been crying out to God to do just that. To search my heart, to help me open myself completely to him, to challenge my motives. I've not always liked what I've seen about myself after such prayers, but I sense I am growing because of it. And isn't that my goal? To *grow* there from here? Isn't it yours?

4. "Solitude is the place of purification and transformation, the place of great struggle and the great encounter."

—Henri J. Nouwen

Can there be a great encounter with Christ without a great struggle concerning purification and transformation? If there is, let me know. From my very first encounter with Christ (as a young child, when I realized my sinfulness and his righteousness) every meaningful experience with him has eventually been about (or at least included) being transformed into his image. It's been painful at times, but worth my willingness to be conformed to his standard.

5. "[Solitude] is the place where Christ remodels us in his own image and frees us from the victimizing compulsions of the world."—Henri J. Nouwen

Remodeled? Ouch! Quite a unpleasant experience for a self-made, self-modeled Christian. Worldly opinions are shaken, personal weaknesses made more obvious, secular motivations identified and purged. Listen, my friend, I guarantee you that a makeover session at a beauty salon may seem like a lot more fun, but it all washes off at bedtime. The quiet time beautification process lasts forever!

6. "Solitude leads to the awareness of the dead person in our own house and keeps us from making judgments about other people's sins."—Henri J. Nouwen

There's nothing like being alone with God to make me face my own self and my own narrow judgments! Sitting silently in the presence of a holy God is a humbling experience. It makes the whole world outside seem so different as the person inside me changes. Nouwen goes on, "Solitude molds self-righteous people into gentle, caring, forgiving persons who are so deeply convinced of their own great sinfulness and so fully aware of God's even greater mercy that their life itself becomes ministry."

7. "Silence guards the inner heat of the life of the Holy Spirit within us. It is the discipline by which the inner fire of God is tended and kept alive. Silence is a quality of the heart that can stay with us even in our conversation with others. It is a portable cell that we carry with us wherever we go. From it we speak to those in need and to it we return after our words have born fruit."

—Henri J. Nouwen

Silence? Solitude? Quietness? In *my* full-to-bursting life and schedule? Yes. In your day, in my day—quiet and a brief moment of privacy in the presence of God. Unthinkable? Perhaps. Unreasonable? To our way of thinking, maybe. Impossible? No. It might be difficult, even awkward to rearrange our schedules and set our alarm clocks to an earlier hour, but women of strength make the effort until it becomes habit.

Create your own Quiet Time Square.

You can create your own habit of privacy, separation, and recess from the stresses of your daily life and routine; a place and space to take refuge from secular assaults on your senses; a cloister in which you can meet with God and God alone. Make room for the meditations of your heart, for the study of God's Word, and for giving yourself daily to him.

What you will need.

You will need your Bible, a note pad or journal, a pen or pencil, and a quiet place.

Become aware of God.

Become aware of God and of his presence with you. He stands ready, not only to meet with you, but to actually love you as well as guide and direct you. "When ... the Spirit of truth [the Holy Spirit] comes, he will guide you into all truth."[7]

How does God come to you? Jack Hayford says it like this:

A moment in his presence, a moment lost in praise. Sometimes that's all it takes. Just a moment or two ... to clear away the fog, to give you perspective, to melt away the anxiety. To erase the hurry/worry lines from your face. To refill your empty cup.[8]

Begin with a prayer.

A brief prayer and a few moments of reflection are a great way to begin. You might want to thank God for his special blessings to you, and for being there with you now. Tell him that you are thrilled with being with him and the fact that he will meet with you, speak to you, and reveal his will to you through this quiet time. Personalize, and pray to God in your words Jeremiah 29:13-14. For example:

Thank you, dear heavenly Father, that your Word promises that when I seek you, I will find you—that when I seek you with all my heart, you're ready and willing to be found. I seek you now. I give you my whole heart, my day. These moments, here—now, are for you and me, alone.

Read a passage of Scripture.

Read a passage of Scripture that you've already picked out, or begin in the Psalms. Read the Bible as a book to enjoy. Let the words of its pages flow over and into your heart. Do not read simply to understand. Read with openness and receptivity. You are "feeding" on God's word. It is spiritual food to you. "Man does not live on bread alone, but on every word that comes from the mouth of God."[9]

Take time to take it in. You will not understand everything you read. Don't let that bother you. Whisper to God, "I don't get all of this—but I know you will help me understand as we move along. But for now, dear Lord, here in your presence let me *absorb* your Word. Let it be life to me."

Let your reading be broken up by moments of prayer and meditation. In other words, enjoy this spiritual meal. Taste it. Savor it. Read parts of it aloud and listen to how it sounds with differing emphasis. Let your conversation with the Lord Jesus be as intimate as if you were sharing a cup of tea with a close friend.

Write it down.

Write down whatever comes to you during this time so that you will begin to crystalize and capture the actual workings of the Holy Spirit in your heart, mind, and soul. Make it quite personal and direct—not simply what the passage *means*, but what it means *to and for you*. Perhaps the Scripture will trigger some thought not directly related to the passage you are reading. That's all right.

Write it down. Use the chart below as an example to show you how to record your thoughts, what the Lord impresses on you, and what you share with him in return. Eventually you will be able to see how the Lord personally spoke to you. What you put down will become a cherished record of God's personal dealings with you.

Quiet Time Notes
Date: Scripture Reference:
The Lord is impressing on me…
I have shared with the Lord…

(Note: Keeping your sections for writing small tends to encourage clarity of thought and is much more helpful for future reference.)

Close with a prayer.

Pray with thanks, praise, and adoration. Confess any sins that have been revealed to you during this time, asking God's forgiveness and cleansing. Ask him to help you conform both your inner and outer life according to his Word. Affirm your faith in God. Declare your belief in what the Lord has shown you from his Word. For example:

> "God, you are my refuge and my strength."
> "Lord Jesus, I know that you are alive and that your kingdom will surely come; let it come to me today."
> "I can do all things through Christ who strengthens me."
> "You, O Lord, are my Shepherd. You lead me, protect, and feed me. Even my thoughts are blessed when your name crosses my mind."

Tell God how his Word has specifically challenged you to change and grow. You might want to say something like:

> "I choose to let you be my defender and refuge today, Father. I see where I've developed an immediate response of self-defense. Today I ask you to let me know whenever I stop relying on you and start relying on myself."

> "Lord, I choose to let your kingdom live in me today. I pray that you will show me where I am most apt to choose the worldly kingdom in my attitudes, words, and thoughts, and help me refocus my choices on you and your Word."

"Dear Jesus, I choose to live like a victor, enabled by you to face any difficult and even seemingly impossible task. Show me, dear Lord, when I take on the victim role and help me remember who you are in me and who I am in you."

"Lord, you are truly my Shepherd. Help me abandon my own stubborn, self-determined pathway, and get back on the pathway to peace that you offer."

Then wait.
Wait in quietness.
Wait, drinking in God's presence and nearness.
Wait, without hurrying—enjoy.
Wait, heart to heart with the Living God.

Pastor Jack Hayford said, "Intimate time with him during the course of your week can change the way things look in your life. Moments in his majestic presence remind you of the brevity of life, the depth of eternity, the availability of his power, the nearness of his love."[10]

Listen to Henri J. Nouwen's beautiful words:

... standing in the presence of God and with the mind in the heart; that is, at that point of our being where there are no divisions or distinctions and where we are totally one. There God's Spirit dwells and there the great encounter takes place. There heart speaks to heart, because there we stand before the face of the Lord, all seeing, within us.[11]

If we are serious about becoming women of strength, we'll stop as often as we can at Quiet Time Square. We'll let the busy-ness of our lives whirl all around this center of quiet and reverie. In other words, we'll start the business of the day by centering our lives securely in his.

Strong Woman Pitfall Warning!

How sad to meet someone who has taken the time and made the effort to have a daily quiet time each and every day of her busy life, but goes away from that time with the attitude, "There! I've given God this part of my day, the rest belongs to me." The quiet time is only one area of communication and one part of our relationship with Christ. The rest of the day develops other levels of relationship with him to the direct proportion that he is included in them.

✓ Checkpoint:

Describe your present experience and quiet time routine. And if you don't have a quiet time routine, plan one and begin first thing tomorrow.

How could you make this experience better and more fulfilling?

What are the obstacles to your quiet time? How could you overcome them?

12

Prayer Pulloff

Often superhighways pass through cities slightly above them on elevated highways or down below them in tunnels. Usually both sides of the freeway have huge cement walls, sound barriers, and sight blockers. Sometimes you can drive completely "through" a city and never "see" the city. From the expressway you can't get a sense of the city or its people.-Driving on the expressway through a city is kind of like life—sometimes we're so busy going through it, we don't see much of it at all.

As a woman of strength in the making, it will be essential in your journey from "here" to "there" that you take a rest stop at Prayer Pulloff. In addition to our designated quiet times, these are the momentary little diversions from the everyday traffic of life when we pull off, sometimes to take in a spiritual "Vista Point" or just a little side road for a short time of prayer. What I'm referring to here is becoming a woman of prayer.

When I observe women of strength, women whose lives merit a closer look, I discover that they are without exception women given to prayer. Personal prayer. They are women of faith who keep their lives and relationships alive and vital through prayer. They are diligent in prayer. Disciplined in prayer.

And, those I know well seem mostly to center their prayers on present trials, today's needs. E.M. Bounds says it like this:

Bread, for today, is bread enough. Bread given for today is the strongest sort of pledge that there will be bread tomorrow. Victory today, is the assurance of victory tomorrow. Our prayers need to be focused upon the present. We must trust God today, and leave the morrow entirely with him. The present is ours; the future belongs to God. Prayer is the task and duty of each recurring day—daily prayer for daily needs.[1]

Every day has its own demands, and requires its own prayers. Prayer is a today thing. Leave tomorrow with its cares, troubles, and concerns in God's hands. Pray for today. There will be another little prayer path tomorrow.

I've also noticed that women of strength have cultivated a *desire* to pray. Obediently responding to God's inner urgings, they know that God's presence is waiting and they answer willingly to calls of prayer. Perhaps a need, or an immediate question triggers the opening of their hearts toward God, but these women of strength never forget that he is the one who initiates such encounters.

Women of strength don't hesitate to bring their smallest concerns as well as their heaviest responsibilities before the Lord. They meander down their little prayer paths, even if it's only in front of the living room window with a cup of tea, and they pause. They listen more than they speak. They reflectively open their hearts and wait to hear God speak to them with an idea or inner knowing. Content with only an insight, or a hint toward a solution, they are confident that the whole answer will come, even if it sometimes comes slowly.

Women of strength accept the discipline of prayerful listening, unhurriedly giving themselves to the Lord as they discover his will for the specific instances of their lives. They are able to discern the illumination of Scripture and its application to their lives and their deep inner prayers. They accept the fact that while there is no shortcut to holiness, prayer is the sure pathway. It is a well-worn footpath that each one must travel for herself. But most of all, women of strength urge us to believe that prayer is a dialogue between our souls and our Savior—a conversation between two people who dearly love each other.

Is prayer a sidetrack for you? A detour from your busy, important tasks? Or is it an essential rest stop along the way—to be used only when you need it?

I urge you to make prayer the fabric of your life—to weave all kinds of prayer into your day and busy schedule. Begin your morning with prayers of submission and commitment to the Lord. Daily devotional prayers should include thanksgiving, praise, petitions, even prayers of tears. Let your bedtime routine include prayers of trustfully placing yourself and your loved ones into God's hands for the night. I encourage you to address your concerns with the strength you receive from intermittent daily prayers. Take time as you speed down the freeway of life today to make these little spiritual rest stops again and again, until you have given your complete self and total heart over to God. Practice prayer until you are a woman given to prayer—any time, all the time.

Learn to Be Still

When my children were very young, our church was small and there weren't the nursery facilities that are available today. I sat with one child on my lap, one between me and my husband, and one on the other side. I didn't get much out of many services, but eventually my children grew up and some of their earliest and fondest memories are of being in church as a family.

I didn't wait to teach them to be quiet until we were in church, I made it a discipline of my midweek activities to sit quietly with them. Taking them on my lap, we whispered secrets to each other and learned to hold very still. What I did with them during those midweek "stillnesses" trained them for church. But more than that, it trained me as well. It trained me to take moments of quietness and stillness—to let things go for those few minutes of *being* rather than *doing*. It's a practice I maintain today. To hold perfectly still whenever I can, no music, no television or radio; just quietness, stillness, calm, and peace. When I am still, I open my mind and heart toward God. I lean into him much like my children leaned into me.

When you take your little jaunts down Prayer Pulloff, find a place to sit. Teach yourself how to hold so still that your prayers are barely above a mental whisper. Let your spirit reach out to a waiting and loving God. And in an inner, secret place just *be* in his presence.

Keep Your Hands Off

My mother often took us shopping. With five little ones in tow, she walked us through the delightful aisles of Woolworth's or the supermarket in town. "Look," she'd say. "Look all you want, but don't touch." When we forgot, she'd notice immediately and would nod her head. We knew what to do. We were expected to put our hands in our pockets or clasp them behind our backs.

In times of prayer, I have often felt the same kind of knowing nod from God about my direction in life. It carries that same message as the look in my mother's eyes. "You're touching things you shouldn't. Put your hands in your pockets."

It's so tempting to work on things, to touch circumstances and manipulate situations even when we've prayed prayers of surrender and release to God. But when we become women of prayer, when our lives are virtually saturated with all kinds of prayers, we'd best keep our hands in our pockets. We must refrain from touching what we have committed to God for keeping. When you pull off the highway of life to a place of prayer, learn to hold perfectly still. Put your hands in your pockets or fold them quietly in your lap while you enjoy respite in his presence. Idle prayers? Yeah, idle. Idle, warm, peaceful, restful, calming, lovely moments in the presence of God. Doing nothing but loving him and letting him love you. How long has it been since you did that? Women of strength make it a habit.

Strong Woman Pitfall Warning!

One of the most subtle abuses of an active prayer life is the manipulative approach to controlling others because we are "more given to prayer than others."

How many times have you heard a strong woman stop all conversation and discussion with, "But I have prayed much about this, and...." Or, "I've been on my face before God about this and he told me ..." Or the popular phrase in my circles: "I have a check in my spirit about this and ..."

The sad part of this discussion is, of course, that maybe she *has* been much in prayer about the subject or circumstance in question. Perhaps she *was* on her face before God, and I believe in the very real dynamic of God's gentle inner nudge we call a check in the spirit. The real problem comes when the strong woman uses those spiritual-sounding cliches to get her own way, to promote her own agenda, or to manipulate others into submitting to her direction or leadership.

What I'm warning of is this: when you *grow* into a woman of strength, there will come a time when the Lord will show you something different, a better way, a clearer indication of his will. But when that happens, women of strength aren't afraid to hesitate, back off, and wait for him to give others the same internal indications and to pray for that end.

What can be perceived as an open challenge for a strong woman in such a situation is interpreted by a woman of strength as a test of her trust in God to speak to others as clearly as he speaks to her. She deepens her joy that he does so.

✓ Checkpoint:

What part does prayer play in your everyday life?

How does continual prayer express itself in your daily activities?

Are you more apt to bring your smallest details or your heaviest burdens to the Lord in prayer? Why?

When are you more likely to ask someone else to pray for you than to pray for yourself? Why?

How can you make prayer habits the fabric of your life?

13

Discipline Drive

There's no getting around it—women of strength are disciplined women. They are women who have taken the time and effort necessary to grow the fruit of the Spirit that is self-control.[1] Such women have found direction and challenge from God's Word such as found in 2 Peter 1:5-8:

> Make every effort to add to your faith goodness; and to goodness, knowledge; and to knowledge, self-control; and to self-control, perseverance; and to perseverance, godliness; and to godliness, brotherly kindness; and to brotherly kindness, love. For if you possess these qualities in increasing measure, they will keep you from being ineffective and unproductive in your knowledge of our Lord Jesus Christ.

"Most of us," says author Dale Hanson Bourke, "have a negative feeling about the word *discipline*. It sounds so rigid and boring. It reminds us of childhood, when we were 'disciplined' if we were bad. As adults, unfortunately, it's hard to realize that discipline brings with it rewards—a *healthier* trimmer body, more productivity, and even better relationships. Perhaps we could look at the concept more positively if we stopped calling it discipline and started calling it control."[2] (italics mine)

God is serious about us, his children. He is serious about conforming us to the image of his Son, Jesus Christ, and to his holiness. Jerry Bridges says that God will use discipline to bring us to that image.[3] I say he will use very common things in our lives to bring us into discipline. He'll use our busy schedules, the abundance of food, our secret ambitions, our hobbies, and even our closest relationships. All can be tools in the hands of a merciful discipliner when surrendered to him.

If you and I are ever to grow into women of strength, it will be because we choose to be disciplined. We'll let God discipline us whenever he sees the need, and we'll discipline ourselves because of our commitment to be women of strength. It's not popular in our day of trivialities and entertainment-oriented society to be sober-minded. With a wallet full of credit cards and offers of "no-payments-until-next-year," it is hard to be self-restrained and careful. With calendars and daily schedules packed almost beyond our ability to keep every appointment and activity, it's easy to slip and lose our patience and become intolerant of anyone or anything that threatens to interrupt our momentum. Cool, calm, and collected are words that seem to refer to either strong, in-control people, or to unproductive and boring people. The restraint of common sense and well thought through level-headedness can almost seem like qualities of a life devoid of spontaneity.

Yet, look at the women of strength you admire. Notice their sedateness and stability. Observe how many church and social activities they bypass and which ones they attend regularly. Women of strength are self-controlled women. Disciplined. Successful managers of their time and their lives.

How can *you* attain such discipline?

Admit your need to God and to yourself.

Ask the Lord to teach you how to be a disciplined person. Search a concordance and find as many Bible passages as you can that deal with being self-controlled and disciplined. Make a list of the qualities or characteristics that you find in those Bible passages. Ask yourself if you have those qualities and then pray about what you might have to change, manage better, or restrain to become a disciplined woman.

Choose a new definition of what it means to be disciplined.

Banish the idea of discipline as punishment and welcome dreams of presence of mind, steadiness, and optimism. Choose to see discipline as your way of growing up in areas and ways you never gave thought to before. Let it do its work within you as you learn how much discipline *isn't* a part of your daily habit and routine.

Take on only what you can manage.

How many of us have sabotaged our own money-saving or time-management efforts, or weight loss or exercise plans by going from one extreme to another? How much more successful would we be if we took things a bit slower, strengthening boundaries and tightening restrictions little by little? I'm afraid that we've become so used to instant response, immediate results, and sudden success that we jump in feet first, not taking into consideration that the idea isn't to control our money, time, or weight, but to control ourselves. It's not that we take certain areas under discipline, but that *we* become disciplined. The results have to be measured inwardly—in strength, not achievement or performance. Without discipline, we may save a little money, have a little more time, lose a little weight, but if our inner character isn't strengthened in the process, have we really gained all that much?

Give yourself time to become disciplined in habit and daily practice.

Dale Bourke reminds us that once discipline is in place, it's a response that is never thought about or analyzed.

You see, discipline is an inner issue that has influence upon many outer areas. When one is disciplined, there is a power over oneself. A disciplined woman can restrain herself when necessary. She has the fortitude to say "no" to certain things, and "yes" to others with composure and with a reserve of inward strength. Eating, money, homemaking, dependability, and punctuality are all affected by our willingness to submit to discipline.

I've been told that it takes three weeks to break a bad habit and another three weeks to be comfortable with a new, good habit. That's six weeks! Forty-two days. In less than two months, you can actually be comfortable with a trimmed-down schedule, a tighter budget, doing without your credit cards, or refusing dessert. In just under six weeks you could be having a regular daily quiet time and feeling as if it is what brings life to you rather than just being an interruption in your day.

To begin, start small.

We already brush our teeth, take our vitamins, and our medicines, don't we? We wash our clothes, make our beds, and go to work or volunteer positions when scheduled. We already have a certain level of discipline in place. Now it's time to move to a new, deeper level.

Determine to read a portion of Scripture or use a Bible study or devotional guide four or five mornings a week. If you're a regular church attender, give yourself Sunday mornings off from your new devotional discipline. If you want better control of your eating, discipline one food group at a time. For example, add more fruit and fresh veggies before you deny yourself something less healthy. Choose to eat more poultry and fish and automatically reduce the amount of red meat you consume. Decide on personal spending policies, or places where you will and will not eat before you address tougher money or eating issues.

Let discipline build your inner strength in the same way you would condition your body with exercise.

Be reasonable. Don't expect to qualify for the Women of Strength Olympics within a few months. It takes years of determination and commitment to grow into a world-class athlete; you won't become a disciplined woman overnight. Let yourself walk before you make yourself run.

Don't be discouraged, even with the most frustrating relapses.

"I'll never make it!" is not a part of a woman-of-strength-in-training's vocabulary. Just promise yourself you'll keep trying. Promise that as a woman of discipline you won't give up on becoming everything God wants you to be. Determine that when you fall, you'll pick yourself up, dust yourself off, and keep going. Remember, failure is only momentary, but not fatal unless you allow it to be.

Remind yourself often of your successes.

To the casual visitor, the framed book covers on my wall may seem somewhat egocentric, even prideful. But the truth is, not many people come to my writing studio, and I need the daily reminders that I have finished self-discipline-driven projects. Sometimes I need to pick up a handful of letters from my readers to remind myself that what I have done has made a difference. My college diploma that hangs with the book covers makes me remember the discipline it took to finish college. It encourages me to keep studying and learning even harder things than I learned in college.

Remember the promise of God's Word.

Here is a promise from God's Word:

> For if you possess these qualities in increasing measure, they will keep you from being ineffective and unproductive in your knowledge of our Lord Jesus Christ.   2 PETER 1:8

Isn't that something you've noticed about women of strength? They are effective and productive in their knowledge and service for Christ. Isn't that something you long to see in yourself? Then pick an area that needs discipline and let self-control begin its work within you.

Strong Woman Pitfall Warning!

Strong women have a way of wanting to impose on others the areas of discipline they have accepted for themselves: the latest diet craze, multi-marketing scheme, clothing fad, even the seminars they attend, the books they read, and the way they pray. You can watch for this pitfall in your own life by listening to your attitudes. Check your heart if you hear yourself even thinking thoughts like:

everybody needs to read this book, *all* the ladies should go to hear this speaker, *the whole church* should watch this video.

Does this mean you will never again recommend a book, speaker, or seminar? Of course not. Just pick your words carefully. I'm usually suspect that I'm facing a *strong woman* when invitations and suggestions are given as mandates and *musts*.

✓ Checkpoint:

In what areas could you be more disciplined?

What could God do for you that would help you move in a more disciplined direction in this particular area?

How much mercy do you show toward yourself when you fail at something you'd rather be disciplined in?

How do you feel toward people who are more disciplined than you? How do you treat those people?

How do you feel toward people who are less disciplined than you? How do you treat those people?

If you were to take on a new discipline, what manageable discipline might that be?

14

Reclamation Road

I met Beth on the fourth anniversary of her husband's untimely death. This man she had dearly loved self-destructed with drugs and alcohol. Until his death, Beth had managed life as best she could. Suddenly, when he died, all sorts of painful memories swept through her mind. Nightmares followed, and grief-work took its toll. You see, Beth had suppressed a history of child molestation. She had put her past safely away during her married life, but it all resurfaced in the very first days, weeks, and months of widowhood. At the very worst time, Beth was forced to retrace the painful steps of her past—a past she didn't want to remember, but one she couldn't avoid any longer.

It was a long and tedious process of confrontation, forgiveness, and healing, but eventually with the care and guidance of a Christian counselor Beth began to put the pieces of her life back together with Christ's help. Cycles of grief, anger, and resignation kept her on an emotional roller coaster for several years. But when at last the picture puzzle of her life was nearly complete, Beth looked on it to find not tragedy, but triumph. She was beginning to see how much she had actually survived.

A new understanding of herself began to emerge, as did a

completely new woman. For the first time in her life she began to define herself as a victor, not a victim. She chose to look at her past as something she had come through. Something positive was born out of her pain. She realized that all she had come through had given her strength.

Painful? Of course. Fatal? Not on your life! Looking back on her past, Beth realizes she can survive the worst life can throw at her, and now she has the opportunity to *grow* on from here. For those of us surrounding her at this season in her life, she is a marvel—a living example of what the love and mercy of Jesus Christ can accomplish in a heart fully yielded to him.

Judy, my friend of twenty years, was the child of an alcoholic father and a weak, compliant mother. She remembers fear-filled days of hiding from her father's drunken rages. She has memories of crouching in the dirt under the back porch and running away at a moment's notice—winter or summer—to get away from his violent temper. Hers was the textbook model of a dysfunctional family. She could have been scarred for life, but she isn't. Instead she's become a survivor with a point of reference. Many times through the years I've heard her say, "If I could get through that, I can get through anything." I've seen her square her shoulders and repeatedly commit her way to the Lord. "If God took care of me then, he'll take care of me now."

I have my own history of painful childhood experiences. I was extremely unhappy all through my elementary school years. I started first grade at the age of five because there was no kindergarten available. I had to fit into reading, math, and social groups beyond my level of maturity. Intellectually I was fine, but emotionally I couldn't take the battering that came my way.

I was tormented by the older boys in the one-room schoolhouse. The teasing escalated and the taunting increased until I was in tears every day. Even my own cousin was part of the terrible situation that dragged on until I moved away five-and-a-half years later. I must say I played the part of the victim well. Afraid that what they said might be true, I wouldn't tell my parents, even when asked repeatedly why I was so unhappy. When we moved because of my father's job, I left the teasing behind, but I carried the damage done to my self-esteem to my new home.

My early childhood experiences made staying in school difficult. The difficulty was compounded by the separation of my parents and yet another relocation during my high school years. Graduation from high school was a relief. I married young and then tried to go back to school. Entering a classroom was almost unbearable. The pain of childhood dogged me whenever I pursued any education except through independent study.

I came to a crisis point when I had to go for my first parent-teacher conference for my daughter. The hated smells of the classroom—paper, chalk, and paste—forced me to revisit the depths of my pain. What happened to me at five should never have happened, but it did. Children can be very cruel, especially when teachers are overworked and needy children are overlooked.

With the help of my mentor and friend, Barbara, I decided to reclaim those painful days. After all, I decided, this is my life, and that was the only childhood I will ever get. With much prayer and many tears, I took back my past from the bullies. I found a way to reclaim the waste products of those terrible years and transform them into something useful. I refused to disown or surrender any of those days or events, but kept them instead as a part of my life.

Barb helped me to see that no matter how difficult those experiences were, life is precious—too precious to throw away even one day of it. Even those days that were most painful to me.

In retrospect, I can see that the abuse of those early childhood days has actually helped make me what I am today. I learned to play alone. That led to my being able to study alone. It was an important push toward helping me develop my imagination and creativity. By creating imaginary playmates, and even little towns or communities, I developed an active creative side. Those bullies restricted my ability to reach out, so I reached in. There I discovered the wonder of my own thoughts and dreams. I established internal convictions. I believe my negative experiences with them made me better equipped to deal with the peer pressure of the teenage years because I had been vaccinated against the fear of rejection.

Now, as an adult, I work alone. Writing is mostly a solitary career. Am I monastic? Certainly not. I don't live in a vacuum. I have strong, lasting friendships, my family, and church relationships. I think the pain-filled experiences of my early years have taught me to place a high value on good, faithful relationships.

But most important, I have learned not to give my personal power or personal definition of worth to victimizers. I have learned to be a transcendent person—one who knows those boys were wrong. They had to find a victim—someone too young to know better, someone less experienced than themselves. And while I've grown past their abuse, I wonder if they ever did.

You have a story too. Almost everyone has some pain from the past. All women carry inner lacerations from deep disappointment. Many bear ugly scars on their hearts from inconceivable pain and unspeakable mistreatment. Some have been victimized by horrible abuse. Maybe you have known the terror of emotional or even physical abandonment by a parent or spouse. Maybe you have experienced verbal, physical, or even sexual abuse and betrayal by a father, mother, or other family member. Some women have even been victimized by those men whom they trusted who claimed to have "spiritual authority."

And yet, you must remind yourself this: whatever your past, this is your life—filled with both good and bad experiences. Your life is precious—and so are you! You can reclaim your life, in the name and power of Jesus Christ.

Reclamation: Recovering Useful Materials from the Waste Products of Our Lives

Someone once said, "Trash can become a cherished heirloom when carefully restored."

We are becoming an environmentally-conscious society. In our household, we take aluminum cans and plastic bottles and bags to the recycling center. We reuse paper bags and glass jars whenever possible. Empty coffee cans with plastic lids end up holding something or other in the garage or pantry. Believe it or not, I even combine dryer lint and cardboard egg cartons to make wonderful fire starters for our wood-burning stove. All this recycling is done with minimal effort on our part. We've just put a few new habits in place that, over time, have become part of our regular routine.

When you are serious about becoming a woman of strength, you become a recycler of your pain and damaged past. You turn the garbage of your past into something useful. You transcend. You grow. You let the Lord teach you how to forgive. You allow him to give you back what was stolen from you. You allow him to return to you your innocence, value, and wholeness. With his help you can stop letting your past steal from your precious present and damage your yet uncharted future.

You let him not only be the Redeemer for your soul, but also for your life—your entire life.

The Lord Jesus Christ, our Redeemer, Messiah, Prince of Peace, and the ideal man, wants to be your Counselor, Comforter, and personal Good Shepherd. The Man of Sorrows wants you to know he bore your pain. The Crucified One took the sins of your past, the ones you committed and the ones committed against you, to the cross, upon himself. He wants you to know him.

He has paid the price so that your past can once again belong to you, not to those who stole it from you. He paid the mortgage on your sin and settled your account in full. He paid the ransom note completely so that you can be returned to a whole, healthy life. He alone has the power to help you change your pain from something that uses and wastes your life into strength for the glory of God. He longs for your past to give you strength instead of stealing it from you. Only he can give you the courage to turn and embrace your pain-filled past and stop running once and for all.

Larry Crabb said, "People who embrace their hurt are able to pursue God more passionately. And their passion is contagious. Less passionate people can instruct others in biblical living, but only people filled with passion can draw others into biblical relationships."[1]

I might say much the same thing in this way: Only those courageous women who will embrace their hurt are able to pursue God passionately. Those women filled with a passion for becoming women of strength must and will reclaim their entire lives; they will face, then embrace, their pain.

David Seamands wrote,

Remember that Christ is alive. He is here now. And because he transcends time, he is also back at that painful experience. Confess to him, turn over each experience, each emotion and attitude. Let him love and comfort and forgive you. Let him cleanse your hates and comfort your hurts and disinfect your lusts and remove your fears. Then specifically forgive others their trespasses as he also forgives you. Let Christ's love take the place of hate. Let Christ's strength take the place of hurt feelings and self pity. Don't be in a hurry. Allow plenty of time for undisturbed, unhurried prayer.[2]

Take a stroll down memory lane; it's an important part of growing down Reclamation Road. Nobody's asking you to move back to memory lane and take up residence there. You've come too far for that. But with such redirected focus, you can *grow* there from here.

"The ultimate work here," Seamands also says, "is not simply relief from the pain of the past or some level of mental and emotional health, but a growth in Christlikeness and a maturing work of sanctification and true holiness."[3]

The perfect picture of a woman of strength!

Strong Woman Pitfall Warning!

I met a woman recently who had suffered unbelievable abuse as a child, a couple of hurtful relationships in college, and at least one failed marriage in her early thirties. Now married for the second time, she makes everyone around her miserable. Dominating her husband, interfering with her grown stepchildren, she has very openly stated her intention of maintaining control. Why? Because of her pain-filled background, she has chosen the life of the strong woman. Decidedly, she keeps her upper-handed approach to life and family for one reason: she never wants to be hurt again. The only insurance policy she knows, she chooses to dictate out of her fear of being dictated to. She dominates, fearing that if she doesn't she'll be dominated again. Her style of overcoming isn't just stepping above her problems, but stepping on everyone in her pathway whether they were part of her past problems and pain or not. (Note: Sometimes the only way out of our pain is to consult a Christian counselor to work through the issues that cause us to manipulate and control others.)

We're all vulnerable to this pitfall and if we're not extremely careful, we'll get sucked into the quicksand of self-protection, and be held down by our intensive efforts to prevent further pain in our lives.

No one likes pain but only as we give it to God can he use it to transform us into women of strength.

✓ Checkpoint:

In thinking about a past pain-filled situation, have you ever asked God what he would like to create in you because of your pain? If you were to pray such a thing, how would that change the situation?

How would taking that approach change you?

When I say, "embrace your pain," what is your initial reaction?

How does this reaction change when you think about it in terms of something God can use to make you more like Christ if you surrender it to him?

What are some issues, areas, or hurts that you have given over to someone else that you'd like to reclaim?

How would your life change if you did that?

How would doing that change you?

15

Problem Pass

I checked my side-view mirror, stepped on the accelerator, and squeezed my way into the busy, pre-rush hour freeway traffic. Finding an opening, I worked my way over to the fast lane and settled into the traffic flow. I glanced at the clock on the dash. *Two forty-five,* I mused. *Plenty of time.*

Traffic moved smoothly along, and my daughter and I picked up our conversation about her impending wedding and the success of our shopping trip. Rounding a curve in a narrow pass, I saw red taillights brighten as drivers for nearly five miles responded to a sudden crisis situation ahead. I braked and glanced in the rearview mirror, hoping everyone behind me would do the same.

We had carefully planned our shopping day, knowing just when we'd have to be on the freeway to avoid the Los Angeles rush hour crush. I needed to get ahead of the clog in the freeway system in time to make it to an important meeting at church—where I was the person in charge, no less.

Tragedy brought the freeway traffic to an abrupt halt, curtailing the evening plans of everyone stuck there with us. In the pass ahead, a small airplane had plummeted from the sky straight into an eighteen-wheel, fully loaded truck. Pilot, passenger, and truck driver were all dead at the scene. An explosion sent a fire racing up the steep hill toward newly built homes on the rim. Emergency vehicles were screaming their way toward the catastrophe. And we waited.

The wreckage spread out over the entire eastbound side of the freeway. And we waited some more. A helicopter appeared and began dumping water on the flames that were licking their way deliciously toward the homes and belongings above. As smoke filled the pass, we closed the sunroof and windows, depending on the car's air conditioner to keep us cool. The car overheated. I turned off the engine, and we waited. We turned on the radio, and waited. The traffic report gave us the details of the accident and the rest of the news. With no place to turn—no available detour—we knew we'd be there a long time. The fifteen-minute trip through the pass was to turn into three or more hours. I wasn't going anywhere until the mess was cleaned up. Not only had traffic come to a complete stop, so had my appointments, my agenda, my busy life. I could do nothing but wait.

Eventually, a single lane was cleared and three packed lanes of traffic merged tediously into one. Slowly we drove through the tragic crash scene and finally onto the open road ahead.

Problems happen. And when they do, they happen at the very worst times. Those people killed didn't plan to die that day. I knew that for sure. Unforeseen problems with a tiny aircraft sabotaged whatever plans they had for the rest of their lives.

It's the same with us. Nobody plans a crisis day or makes room on their month-at-a-glance calendar for a grief appointment. On our way to something or somewhere else, troubles occur. And, it's not always our fault. Sometimes, sure, but not always.

Rarely does an airplane fall out of the sky or spacecraft hardware plunge into your path, but crises happen. And everything changes. Trouble, problems, and tough times come to all of us. Whether they are the result of our own or someone else's carelessness, recklessness, or neglect, troubles are problematic and often severely painful.

Life happens to all of us. Shakeups we didn't ask for—didn't even leave a door open for—bring strife and confusion. Sometimes the unexpected is only a nuisance. At other times it is trauma—a situation that weighs heavily on our heart, saps our energy, and strips our confidence. Shakeups can be bothersome or they can be bewildering.

Once in a while a detour opens up and you get to go around a problem. Sometimes a rescuer comes along and you get taken out of the adversity. But often, like everyone else living now or who has ever lived before, disorder, turbulence, and ordeals come, and like being stuck on the freeway with no way around or out, we go through hard times. Eventually we are on the open road again and on with life.

Women of strength realize that life isn't always going to be smooth sailing. They realize that even our carefully guarded devotional hour and prayer times can be interrupted with an emergency phone call. Problems are not polite; they're invaders, delayers, and sometimes saboteurs. But women of strength look at problems and troubles as opportunities and choices. They look at the delays as having value in serving divine purposes.

My favorite classic author, George MacDonald, says it like this:

Sometimes a thunderbolt will shoot from a clear sky; and sometimes into the life of a peaceful individual, without warning of gathered storm, something terrible will fall. And from that moment everything is changed. That life is no more what it was. Better it ought to be, worse it may be. The result depends on the life itself and its response to the invading storm of trouble. Forever after, its spiritual weather is altered. But for the one who believes in God, such rending and frightful catastrophes never come but where they are turned around for good in his own life and in other lives he touches.

You see, troubles appear without warning or announcement, just like unexpected traffic delays on the freeway. They happen and we have no choice but to wait. And when they do, we have more than just external inconvenience—it is also internal. After all, I wasn't on the freeway that hot day for no reason at all. I was going somewhere. And I was stuck ... right there in the Southern California summer heat ... with thousands of others who were also on their way somewhere. None of us planned for, and few of us prepared for, such a delay.

It's true that I was stuck, at least for the moment, but I was able to choose my attitude toward the situation. I could have stewed and complained, honked my horn, or even have picked a fight with my daughter. The husband and wife in the lane next to us chose to do that. Instead, I chose to relax and enjoy the unexpected few hours of leisure—no phone, no rush—and an unexpected gift of personal time with my soon-to-be-married daughter.

No matter what anyone says, when problems come, interrupting the flow of our regular lives and personal agendas, we choose. We can simmer just under a full boil, we can murmur and criticize, we can blame, pout, and flail about in a temper. We can moan, stage a protest, declare our innocence and the injustice of it all. Or, determined to make the most of every experience of life, we can use problem time to grow, deepen trust, and strengthen faith. As women of strength, we can put difficulty to good use. We can use problems to grow. And we won't even have to go out looking for trouble in order to benefit from it. Trouble always finds all of us. And it comes often enough to help us try again if we fail to make good use of it the first time.

Here are a few things to decide *before* trouble strikes:

- Trouble will come. Guaranteed. Even Jesus said it would (John 16:33).
- Trouble will go.
- Growth can result.

The way I see it, trouble brings with it the unique opportunity to *grow on* with our lives. Trouble challenges our faith, and tests our trust in God. We get to see how much we've learned and how much learning is yet needed. It shows us our strength and reveals our weaknesses. It keeps us on track.

What Scripture Tells Us about Life's Problems

Let's examine some Scriptural principles we can follow when trouble presents itself.

Problems do not mean we're out of touch with God, or that we are beyond God's reach.

Second Peter 2:9 says it like this: "The Lord knows how to rescue godly men from trials." When you are being hassled by difficulties, remember, God is able take you out. But he can also take you *through*. Is either one less than a rescue? Problems can serve both God's purposes and our benefit.

In my book, *Making Sense of Pain and Struggle* I wrote, "The struggles of my life... are the heat that brings the impurities to the surface. God does not *cause* the struggles in my life, but he can use them—if I allow him to."[1]

The struggles I have experienced have brought out my bad attitudes, unforgiveness, selfishness, and pride. The pain of those struggles has caused me to seek Christ at a deeper level. Those struggles have drawn me closer to his Word and to his principles for living. Yes, my problems have often been the very thing that has given me more compassion, patience, and tolerance with others who are struggling. But even more, troubles have often put me in closer touch with God than ever before.

Problems help us grow up.

> Consider it pure joy, my brothers, whenever you face trials of many kinds, because you know that the testing of your faith develops perseverance. Perseverance must finish its work so that you may be mature and complete, not lacking anything.
>
> JAMES 1:2-4

Persevere? Wait? Work it out? How long? I don't like this! We all sing the same mournful song, don't we? I stop at a fast food place, pick up supper at the drive-through, rush home to put in another load of laundry before heading out to a Bible study or committee meeting. I don't have time to develop perseverance! I want to buy it, rent it, or get it at a weekend seminar. But it doesn't come that way, does it? God's Word says it comes through trial, not just one trial, but *trials of many kinds*. Women of strength compare trials to what it takes to grow a prizewinning rose—in other words, manure, deep root feeding, and regular pruning.

Troubles prove whether or not we can "walk the talk."

Now for a little while you may have had to suffer grief in all kinds of trials. These have come so that your faith—of greater worth than gold, which perishes even though refined by fire—may be proved genuine and may result in praise, glory and honor when Jesus Christ is revealed.   1 PETER 1:6-7

A genuine faith? Does one have to have a *proven* genuine faith? Back to the refinery, again? Yes! And again and again, until our purity is as clear as a freshwater lake, one Jesus can see his face reflected in, until our very lives are praise and glory and honor to Jesus Christ. Troubles are the best way to prove anyone's faith. Ease and comfort prove nothing.

Problems can serve God's purposes and our benefit.

Because the patriarchs were jealous of Joseph, they sold him as a slave into Egypt. But God was with him and rescued him from all his troubles. He gave Joseph wisdom and enabled him to gain the goodwill of Pharaoh king of Egypt; so he made him ruler over Egypt and all his palace.   ACTS 7:9-10

Strength is more than the sum total of our troubles and our victories. It's more than our successes weighed against our failures. Strength is godly character developed within us when we choose our responses to both the good and the bad of our lives. It thrives when we trust God enough to know he can work good *in* us, even in the most miserable of our troubles and defeating struggles.

Painful problems can give birth to ministry.

The Bible says:

> The God of all comfort, who comforts us in all our troubles, so that we can comfort those in any trouble with the comfort we ourselves have received from God. For just as the sufferings of Christ flow over into our lives, so also through Christ our comfort overflows.   2 CORINTHIANS 1:3-5

In her wonderful book, *Rose to Brier*, Amy Carmichael speaks of what ministered to her in her extreme physical pain:

> [T]hings written by those who were in pain themselves, or who had passed through pain to peace, like the touch of understanding in a dear human letter, did something that nothing except the words of our eternal Lord could ever do.

Nothing soothes a troubled soul like a friend who has known trouble. Troubles can correct our defective vision.

> Therefore we do not lose heart. Though outwardly we are wasting away, yet inwardly we are being renewed day by day. For our light and momentary troubles are achieving for us an

eternal glory that far outweighs them all. So we fix our eyes not on what is seen, but on what is unseen. For what is seen is temporary, but what is unseen is eternal.

2 CORINTHIANS 4:16-18

In times of trouble, we can look to Jesus, to God's Word, and to a bright and hope-filled future, no matter what our present circumstances dictate or threaten. When things look so bad, God's love looks so wonderful. When all hope is lost, we find hope again in him. In times of ease, we often forget. In trials we remember.

Problems teach us to pray at new levels.

Do not be anxious about anything, but in everything, by prayer and petition, with thanksgiving, present your requests to God.

PHILIPPIANS 4:6

Praying—petitioning with thanksgiving—changes drastically in the face of trouble. We tap into a deeper level of relationship when we reach inside, to our solid relationship with him. In the face of trouble, we are able to lift up thankful hearts—even when an unsaved onlooker would not be able.

✓ Checkpoint:

Recall a time when a problem or sudden trouble brought your life to a sudden halt.

Sometimes our troubles are our own fault, sometimes not. Was the event you listed above your fault, or someone else's? Was it perhaps, like an illness or accident, not anyone's fault?

Looking back, what, if any, choices and opportunities we offered by or during that event.

What attitude did you choose during that difficult period?

__ anger   __ despair   __ prayer   __ revenge
__ faith   __ acceptance   __ resistance   __ denial
__ victim

At this stage in your life, what can you honestly say you learned from that painful time?

How has this situation served to cause you to seek Christ at a deeper level?

What good did God work in you, even in this most miserable trouble or struggle?

16

The Desert Crossing

A lone. *Alone!* I don't know when it happened, exactly, but one day I realized how alone I felt. Abandoned, forsaken. I still had all the people I loved around me. My family was there, everyone was healthy, we had our church. Oh, we had the normal stresses, but nothing catastrophic. For some unknown reason, I felt so all alone.

Furthermore, I discovered that while I was usually a bubbly person, talkative and happy, I was becoming somber—almost moody and withdrawn. Even my walk seemed heavy and my steps hard. Long sighs of contentment while playing with my little girls and looking into the face of my baby son were replaced with deep sighs of bottomless emptiness. My peace and satisfaction in Christ had been disturbed. No longer blissfully happy and fully alive, I doubted God's love and care. Instead of facing each day with a sense of strength and confidence, I felt flat of faith and hopeless.

What could have gone wrong? I had no burdensome chains of the past haunting me. I was sure of my place in God's kingdom. But I could no longer find the strength to reject the accusations of the enemy of my soul. The Bible said I was a conqueror in all things, but I felt defeated.

I found myself under a steady assault of dullness. Life's circumstances seemed to magnify my dis-ease within. Even little problems challenged me with no let up or relief. At first I was determined not to let myself fall under the spell of discontentment and dryness. But my determination wore out and failed.

What can't be overcome with determination, I decided, is best met with defiance. So I swallowed hard, lifted my chin and challenged life head on. I took charge. I proclaimed my position in Christ with words of boldness and authority that immediately fell flat at my feet. Yet, I resisted the temptation to whimper and moan. I stiffened at the idea that I could be backsliding. I stubbornly refused to give in to discouragement, but soon lost the battle and became discouraged.

Instead of "Sonlight in my soul," I discovered shadows across my heart. Restless and irritable, mostly with myself, I spent every effort trying to disguise my condition to others. In faith, I waited for it to pass, all the while pretending it had never come.

A coolness began to invade my soul, and I served God between clenched teeth. Dissatisfied, impatient, and spiritually annoyed, I resented God's apparent lack of interest in me or my problem. Finally one day I admitted my miserable spiritual state to a friend who told me to see a psychiatrist. Confused, lonely, and disturbed in my deepest heart, I wondered if she had a point, but instead I went to prayer, giving God one last chance.

A tumble of confused thoughts and feelings tore from my heart as I gave my spiritual chaos words. I confessed my fears that in some unknown somewhere I'd lost out, that certainly there must be fault someplace deep within my heart. God was obviously mad and must have good reason to keep completely silent.

I tearfully admitted that I was sick of the struggle and ready to give up. My doubtful, disquieted, and troubled soul-searching went on for days and weeks. My eyes were constantly swollen from my tearful prayers of misery. I was bombarded with thoughts of what a failure I was, how useless I was to God or anybody else. I sobbed out how abandoned I felt. I admitted my mind was congested with doubts, fears, worthlessness, and sorrow.

Assessing my Christian life, I discovered a shabby synthetic quality about it. I was spiritually barren and parched. As a Christian I was dead. Stone cold dead. Spiritually I was worn out like an old crocheted dishrag. Things of God had become tiresome, boring, and uninteresting. Reading the Bible was blah, flat, and stale. Words of encouragement rang hollow and dull.

There was no doubt about it, I was certain I had been forsaken by the very One who promised he'd never do that. God not only was neglecting me, but had completely vanished—deserting me. But why? Why would God give up on me? What had I done that was so awful that I deserved to be discarded and left behind?

Was my once lush, rich life in Christ to be nothing more than a distant memory? When had his abounding love stopped flowing in my inner life? Why did God seem so far away? He must be preoccupied with the business of heaven, I decided. He must be engrossed in universal difficulties and lost in thought about other things—certainly not me! Can God be absent? Is he off, far away, somewhere else, not here? It seemed so to me.

"Welcome to Desert Center"

During this miserable time, I took a vacation to my hometown area with my husband and children. Going east on the freeway just outside Palm Springs, we came across a sun-bleached, battered sign punctured with bullet holes reading, *Welcome to Desert Center*. The arrow on the sign seemed to point directly into my heart of hearts, to the deepest, dustiest, most barren part of my dry, wasted soul. In that one moment, as my gaze wandered over the rock-strewn, cactus-littered vista, God began to speak to me.

That was the beginning of my way out. I began to understand that I wasn't crazy or depressed in the clinical sense of the word. I was in a spiritual wilderness—a desert—a dry place. I hated it, and I had no idea what it all meant.

I had spent my earliest childhood in California's Mojave Desert so I was no stranger to arid lands. I hated it then, and I had little regard for it as an adult. We were only there to show the kids where I had lived as a child.

I was familiar with the desolation, the dust, the gusty winds that blew porches off houses and flattened poorly built barns. It was no-man's-land then as now. Even the large rock painted with "Kilroy Was Here" didn't amuse me, although I noted the fact that Kilroy obviously had the good sense to either die or leave, I wasn't ever sure which.

Some of my earliest childhood memories were of lonely days up "on the hill" above Yucca Valley. My sisters and cousin were away in school and my baby brother was too young to play outside. I thought the desert was devoid of beauty and empty. At four years of age, I hated it. At thirty I found myself not living in a physical desert town, but in a spiritual desert. And though my physical home was no longer a desert town, my soul was living in just such a spiritually dry place.

In the more than twenty years since that insightful day, I have been there again and again. And I've known others who have been there too. My friend Judy recalls a six-year desert experience. In fact, I've actually discovered that all God's people at one time or another go through a desert place.

The Deserts of Scripture

From the very beginning, desert-time has been a part of life for God's people. The Bible people actually were desert people—desert travelers, desert dwellers. And all through the Bible, we find that God led, drove, planned for, and met his people in the desert.

If you and I are to grow into the women of strength we deeply desire to be, we must learn to recognize our interior desert. There is value in going through such inner dry places and there is much we can learn from our experiences there. We can find what we need to know about these "deserts" in the Bible.

God takes us into the desert.

One of the most striking scenes in the gospel accounts is Jesus' baptism by John. Immediately following the affirmation of his Sonship, God led him into the desert.[1]

There's no mistaking it. The Holy Spirit took him to the desert. Let's be sure of this: God sent his only begotten Son to the desert; he will surely take us there as well.

God can find us in the desert.[2]

"Where can I go from your Spirit? Where can I flee from your presence? If I go up to the heavens, you are there; if I make my bed in the depths, you are there."[3] Even in the wasteland of our most wild and strange desert experience, even when alone is spelled in large, bold, capital letters across our emotions, we are not hidden from the sight of our loving and caring heavenly Father. He knows and he sees.

God speaks in the desert.[4]

When my family and I lived in the desert near a military training base, I heard a sonic boom for the first time. The thunderous explosion sliced through the silence of the clear blue sky, echoed throughout the valleys, and bounced off the mountain tops. Then, in a split instant, everything fell silent again. It happened so fast it made you wonder if you heard it at all. Suddenly a lizard scrambled as silent as a whisper onto a rock nearby. I jumped, trembling with fear.

But with God's voice, it's a different matter entirely. To Moses God spoke from a mysterious burning bush. Was it as loud as the sonic boom? I don't know. But I know that in the silent desert, any sudden voice can scare you to death.

Elijah had another kind of encounter.[5] Fleeing in fear for his life, the prophet spent the night hiding in a cave. God told the prophet to go out and stand on the mountain top, right in plain sight in the middle of the desert. Elijah did what God told him. The Bible says it like this: "Then a great and powerful wind tore the mountains apart and shattered the rocks before the LORD, but the LORD was not in the wind. After the wind there was an earthquake, but the LORD was not in the earthquake. After the earthquake came a fire, but the LORD was not in the fire. And after the fire came a gentle whisper." (I imagine it was like that lizard silently scampering across the rock.) "When Elijah heard it, he pulled his cloak over his face and went out and stood at the mouth of the cave. Then a voice said to him, 'What are you doing here, Elijah?'"

God's voice doesn't always pierce the desert sky with a booming voice to rival a sonic boom. In the desert, when he has our full attention, he sometimes speaks barely above a whisper. "What's going on?" he asks silently. "Why are you here?" And, in such a moment, with the voice of Majesty whispering your name and mine, we can speak back in much the same tone. "It seems I've lost my direction, Lord. I don't know where I am, for sure. I'm just here in this dry, desolate place."

The Bible records that God told Elijah where to go and what to do. He'll do the same for us. After all, we're *growing on* from here. We're desert travelers, not dwellers, spiritually speaking. We're growing on with him as our guide *through* the desert.

The desert is where we can experience God's tenderness and intimacy at a level unavailable anywhere else.[6]

Without the desert place, we will never be fully strengthened in the same way as when we finally, wisely choose to let God speak to or meet us there. The busy hustle-bustle of our lives can't teach us what the silent, thirsty desert experience can. The high-praise and worship at the most spiritually attuned church can't. The high-pitched camp meeting can't either. Nor can the excitement of a revival. There's so much to be learned by going through desert places with God.

It was in the desert that God told Moses he was standing on holy ground. It's not an experience to be rushed; the desert place is above all, quiet, even silent. There is no hurry, no danger, for the Lord is especially protective of us when we walk there. It is he who is testing us in the desert places, he who will reveal himself to us in a new and distinctive way. He provides our oasis moments in the desert. He disciplines us while we walk there. He humbles us and proves us, and he proves himself as well in those dry, dusty spiritual sojourns.

The desert is part of our inheritance as God's people, and though it is often uncomfortable and strange, it can be as much a place of safety and shelter for us as it was for David when he was hiding from Saul.[7]

Like Elijah, we soon learn that the desert serves as a good place to come to the end of ourselves.[8] When we get to that point, our journey through the desert is almost over. That is the precise and foremost purpose of such experiences. For you see, the desert is widely known as a place of death. In our spiritual deserts, we can find a death to our willfulness, our deceptions, our flesh, and our selfish dreams; our self-centered, self-made plans; and our self-determined purposes. All our best ideas and most noble motivations turn to dust or petrify in the spiritual desert experience. The bones of our pseudo-piety are left to bleach in the desert sun. Remember, I know. I've been there.

When walking through desert places with the Lord, I have discovered cowardice where I thought I had courage. I found unfaithfulness where I would have sworn faithfulness. My impatience, lack of faith, and prayerlessness were uncovered in spiritual desert places. Stubbornness and confusion were exposed, and my true heart was shown to be much smaller and harder than I had secretly boasted. My motivations were tried and found to be weak and self-serving. In other words, I died to myself in the desert. No wonder I hated it. Desert desolation is a graveyard for what the Bible calls the "old man"—the carnal *me* I had to leave behind.

On that trip to my hometown that summer some years ago, I also discovered some things about the beauty of the desert. I found that the place I once considered a wild and strange wasteland also has a clear sky, so blue it can hurt your eyes, and billowy white clouds that float silently overhead. What I used to think of as a blazing desolation I had to somehow cross, I know now as the home of a sunset to rival any display of color I have ever seen. Brilliant magenta slowly metamorphoses into cotton candy pink right before your eyes. Shades of purple and grey stretch long fingers above the rugged mountain silhouettes at twilight. Under a full moon, the Joshua trees are gilded with moonlight. Stars are sprinkled like diamond dust across eternity when the black sky is moonless. Delicate desert roses open each morning and spectacular tissue paper flowers of raspberry, hot pink, bright yellow, and purple bloom each spring amid forbidding spiny cactus needles. After a sudden rainfall the otherwise odorless terrain of the desert breathes with the pungent smell of sage. The smell of desert cedar lingers on both a hand and in a memory, as do sweet and moist wild pinion nuts, belying their dry, waterless habitat. Miniature, frail, yellow butterflies flutter about as if in the most abundant flower garden on earth. Hot springs fed from molten magma churn up from some mysterious place deep within the earth beneath, and cool artesian wells bubble to the surface unannounced.

Driving down a long desert highway, it's not unusual to find a paintless, sandblasted gas station offering cold drinks from a soda pop cooler tucked under and away from the hot rays of midday sun. And don't forget the hidden treasures of the desert. Silver, gold, copper, and other minerals lay buried beneath its dreary facade. And the gemstones! They wait for the experienced eye of the lapidary.

In the same way, our spiritual desert places offer their own special beauty. These places offer the beauty of holiness[9] for the redeemed of God. The desert can be a place of deep refreshment and a place of praise[10] for God's chosen people. Artesian wells of his matchless mercy and grace spring up in unexpected places and in surprising ways. Promises from his Word emerge in full color from the most sticky situations. Memories of God's faithfulness flutter to the surface of our minds, reminding us of his goodness. Cool drinks of encouragement are handed to us by strangers assigned to tend our way.

But the most beautiful of all, is that the desert is the place in which God reveals his Son Jesus Christ to be our very sustenance and life.[11] It is where he reminds us that while we live in the world, we belong exclusively to him.

When at last we leave the desert, and return to civilization once again—to our busy lives and schedules—we begin to understand. We start to see that the purpose of the desert was to simplify, to refine, and to purify our hearts, leaving them bare and empty, a clean place for God to live. Stripped of all unnecessary trappings—even of our spiritual excesses—we are changed because of being in the desert place.

We are different because it's impossible to be or stay the same after such an experience. Transformed, we are more balanced, wiser, and much more inwardly prepared to go on with our lives, fully understanding our utter dependence on God. With a new willing resolve to do things his way we come back renewed, refreshed, and with a deeper understanding of those ways. We have discovered the hidden treasure of new insight into his Word. We are more aware of our treasured place in Christ and his priceless place in us. Knowing our destiny is to rule and reign with him, we also know it is to suffer and learn obedience. In the desert place we discover our utter helplessness, and at the same time, his awesome power.

The desert place is intended for our strengthening—strengthening in faith, understanding, prayer, endurance, perseverance. The spiritual desert place with its strange and foreboding emotional landscape introduces us into intimacy with God. *It* is wild and untamed, but *we* will come out broken and tamed. It is formidable and harsh to teach us of God's approachability and tender heart. It is unfriendly to teach us of God's love. And, my friend, the desert awaits. Unhurried. Unchanging. The inner desert waits for us to visit, to learn, and then to go on. It is a place to revisit as often as necessary to learn about ourselves and God.

Women of strength like us go there, and learn to trust God as never before; we *grow* on from there. Expect to go back to the desert once in a while; for until we see him face to face, we will need the ever-strengthening experiences of the desert.

Preparing for the Desert Crossing

A word of advice lest you think you will faint in the desert. It's a wilderness, that's for certain. But it also has a beginning and an end. The desert experience is but a parenthetical comment in the volume of your life.

Watch for subtle changes in your spiritual life that don't respond to repentance, petition, or intercessory prayers.

When traveling toward the California desert, a transition occurs. Trees get fewer and farther between. Even the soil changes color. The mountains look different, all spotty and freckled with rocks and scrub brush. Tumbleweeds begin to roll across the windy openness and before long you know it. Coming around a curve, or over a mountain summit, there it is—the desert. At this distance you can see the desert begins here and ends on the distant horizon. But when you're in the middle of it, there seems to be no beginning or ending.

And so it is with our inner desert experiences. A subtle transition occurs. The richness of our soul seems to get sparse and dusty, and our inner thirst recognizes the dryness of the spiritual climate. Going further, we come to a particular place or experience that for each of us individually signals the desert threshold. Only an individual can define or determine when or where that is. But the survival skills are common to all. For examples of what I mean read on.

Look for oases in your desert.

There will be oasis-moments as you cross your spiritual desert. Take advantage of those sparsely-placed moments of rest and refuge from the harshness of the desert experience. Many experienced desert travelers will tell you it's foolishness to pass up an oasis. The next one may be a long way off. Don't feel guilty for taking the moment of respite and refreshment offered. Plunge in without reservation. As much as the desert experience is of God, so is the oasis moment.

When you are in your desert and a getaway invitation is suddenly extended, accept it. When your church has a retreat, go. And don't require yourself to attend every meeting if you want to rest. Don't pressure yourself to take up a new craft. This is your oasis. God gave it to you—ask him how to get the most out of it for the journey yet ahead.

Throughout your desert experience, maintain your devotional routine, even if it's dry and unproductive.

Desert experiences almost always yield their insights and revelations later on. It can be easy to abandon your devotional times during dry spells, just when you need them most. When prayer doesn't come easily, spend silent moments before God. Enjoy his presence without the pressure of your performance or productive prayer and Bible study. Instead, meditate on familiar or favorite passages such as Psalms 23, 34, or 37. Perhaps reading a prepared devotional guide that speaks of God's care and concern would be wiser than taking an in-depth Bible course while you're in your desert. Read the words of old hymns or spiritual or Christian poetry to moisturize your dry soul. And, of course, you can review previously underlined passages of Scripture, promises God has made to you in the past. Journalize if possible, if impossible, don't. You won't soon forget what you learn during this time.

Travel light.

You don't go camping in the desert with a perfectly matched designer luggage set packed to the limit. Neither is a desert experience appropriate for fully-packed lives and calendars. Let the exhaustion that brought you to this desert place show you how to simplify your life and schedule. Take a look at present responsibilities and stresses—then unload some or all of them if necessary. Don't take on any new and unnecessary stresses or responsibilities. Refuse them with the simple response, "This isn't the right time." Avoid Christian busywork without feeling guilty.

Reduce your daily routine to a minimum, tending only to basic responsibilities.

Believe it or not, this reduced routine is God's way of helping you survive the desert. If getting up, brushing your teeth, and fixing breakfast is all you can accomplish right now—so be it. On your very next day off, wear your robe until noon—will the world fall off its axis? In other words, let life be easier. Slow down, the beauty of the desert isn't found going down the black-topped superhighway ten miles per hour over the speed limit. No, the beauty of the desert is discovered when you move at the pace of the desert. It is taking the rough, untraveled side roads ... waiting for evening ... marveling at the majestic sunset ... watching each star appear overhead as twilight gives way to dark night.

Strip your routine to its barest. Then sit awhile. This time is too precious to waste with rush.

Verbalize to yourself what you know about God, not what you feel *about him.*

Your feelings about God, your life, or yourself are out of perspective during the desert seasons. Remember, your relationship with him is not in jeopardy simply because you *feel* like it is. You are not wasting your life doing nothing important for him simply because it's how you *feel* at the moment. Even the ugliest horned toad sunning himself on a rock in the desert was created by God and has value. And what's more, that hideous creature lives there all his life. You won't feel like this forever—just while you go through the desert.

Be ready to leave the desert as soon as it ends.

"There it is," God will soon say, "the other side. The promised boundary is in sight." The sparkling image on the distant horizon isn't a mirage, it's life. Full, productive, and overflowing with freshness and vitality. Very soon, signs of life will appear sporadically, then more frequently, and finally fragrant and in full blossom all around you.

You made it! You came *through* Desert Crossing. And may I say, you look absolutely strengthened by the experience! As a friend might say, "Girlfriend, you are the most *growin'* thing I know!"

Strong Woman Pitfall Warning!

Bitterness, despair, and depression are cleverly hidden in many secret places across the desert experiences of our lives. Carefully disguised and covered, doubt waits with its powerful jaws ready to clamp around your heart like a spring-loaded trap awaiting prey.

Check your heart whenever you find your spirit rising up in protest against God and his working in your life. Examine your inner self whenever you feel like screaming against the seemingly brassy heavens above your head.

How tempting it is to take the *strong woman* approach to the desert experiences of life, to simply take matters into our own hands and find the shortest route out of the hot, dusty spiritual void. Sometimes even serving a lesser god would be more appealing than continuing to serve one who seems silent and distant.

But listen up, here! You are a *woman of strength in the making* and you've come so far. This is no time to begin playing around with less than eternal values and lower kingdom issues. Deserts don't last forever. And, even though it seems it will never happen, rains come and streams occasionally flow, even in the driest places.

Believe it or not, the greatest danger of the *strong woman pitfall* isn't in the desert experience itself, but afterward. And it comes in the form of seductive pride. After all, look where you've been and what you've come through. You can even become convinced you deserve to stand a little taller than those who've never been through such a dry place. Look how much God trusted you to lead you there. How impressive that he *grew* you through this challenge, that he thought enough of you to single you out for this season. How grand that he had enough confidence in you to know you'd pass the test and come out triumphant and full of faith.

Careful now, the bright and shiny trap of pride is about to spring. Nothing grabs an unsuspecting person faster than a trap of self-magnificence.

Remember, the desert experience should bring you to the end of yourself, not fill you full of it. Once you get to that point, empty and void, let God fill you with more of himself and his love. Let the experience give you his strength.

✓ Checkpoint:

How do you know that what you're going through is a genuine desert experience?

What possible good can come from desert experiences that bring out the absolute worst in us?

How are you preparing yourself for the desert experiences yet to come?

17

Detour Through Death Valley

It's happened to you. It's happened to me.

The phone rang as I put away the dishes from breakfast. I knew immediately that something was wrong by something in the sound of the voice that greeted me. "Hello, Mrs. Coyle?" the voice asked.

My heart stopped and I held my breath. "Yes?" I answered questioningly.

"I'm calling on behalf of your mother. Frances Stephenson is your mother, right?"

"She is."

"There's been an accident ..." the man paused. "Mrs. Coyle?"

"I'm here," I said numbly.

"She and your dad have been taken to the hospital. She's asking for you."

A crisis. An abrupt halt to my day, my emotions, and my peace. Life brings its challenges and occasionally its crises. I was headed in one direction that day, but ended up somewhere else. And it has happened since.

Without warning I turned a corner I didn't even know was there. Automatically everything is changed, forever. You know what I mean. Knife-sharp words slice through our peaceful lives. Words such as: *Your daughter's neck is broken. Cancer. M.S. We lost the baby. You're fired. He's gone. He's dead. It's over. I want a divorce. Mom, I'm in a little trouble. Ma'am, I'm afraid I have bad news.* And life changes at that very unwanted, dreaded, *unplanned* moment.

Those life-changing moments don't always come from external sources. Once in a while they come from within. *I failed. I hate him! I want out! I want to die! I can't go on. I can't take any more. I quit!*

Death Valley National Park is one of the hottest regions in North America, boasting the highest temperature ever recorded in the United States: 134 air degrees, and 175 on the ground! One old prospector called Death Valley, "Hades with the lid off," and I've been there—you probably have too. Okay, not the actual geographical Death Valley, but I have visited depths of discouragement and despair that left me with a life that could only be described with words similar to the old prospector's—a life that in one fateful moment changed from bad to worse.

The Mojave Desert is punctuated with names and places like Palm Springs, Palmdale, Desert Hot Springs, Yucca Valley, Thousand Palms, and Rancho Mirage. But in Death Valley you find names and places like Black Mountain, Badwater, Funeral Mountain, Stovepipe Wells, Furnace Creek, and Desolation Canyon. These geographical points of interest on a map could well be representative of the crises and points of struggle we experience in our lives.

How "Death Valley Detours" Fit into God's Plan

Thankfully, while life does indeed make sudden changes and leave us breathless and afraid, such moments don't last forever. For Christians, the metaphoric "Death Valley" isn't a destination, it's a detour. And what's more, even though these detours can feel like catastrophic setbacks, as aspiring women of strength we can use them to *help* us toward our goal. These devastating detours come our way anyway, so why not learn to let God use them for our good? Consider what the Bible says in Romans 8:28.

And we know that in all things God works for the good of those who love him, who have been called according to his purpose.

Aren't we determined to be—even *sense* we are called to be— women of strength and purpose? God's purpose? Haven't we learned through our successful passage through problems and emerging victorious from our desert experiences that he does in fact work *in* all things for *our* good? Haven't we cried out to be more like Christ, and to live purposefully and perseveringly for God's kingdom and will?

Crisis moments and experiences change more than our lives, they change us. As long as we're living on this earth, breathing this air, we can be sure that God will continue to take full advantage of every opportunity to change us into the likeness of his Son, Jesus.

For those God foreknew he also predestined to be conformed to the likeness of his Son.   ROMANS 8:29

The Death Valley detours we encounter can serve such a purpose. Let me explain. Death Valley, California, is a geological wonder. Formed ages ago, it is really a cruel cutaway of the earth's interior completely surrounded by mountain peaks of five thousand to over eleven thousand feet, the valley itself is a fault basin. Not unlike the more subtle San Andreas fault that runs the length of California, Death Valley is the wasted historical battle ground of two dueling faults that literally pulled the place apart. When one takes the courageous trek to the bottom of the valley, it is an actual journey into the earth's internal history.

In our own Death Valley detours, it can feel as if the foundations of our lives are being shaken, as if two underlying plates, the very foundations of our lives, suddenly shift deep within. Fear and faith collide. Despair caused by the situation and our hope built on God, smash into each other, struggling for dominance. Wicked pain rumbles against the wonderful promises of God's Word. A battle ensues and rips our lives apart, leaving layers of our personal histories exposed and our tender hearts vulnerable.

At moments like these, verses like Psalm 51:6-8 take on special meaning.

> Surely you desire truth in the inner parts; you teach me wisdom in the inmost place. Cleanse me with hyssop, and I will be clean; wash me, and I will be whiter than snow. Let me hear joy and gladness; let the bones you have crushed rejoice.

When these cataclysmic events occur, even with our entire inner selves ripped wide open, we do well to seek the face of God. Only he knows this Death Valley detour from beginning to end. Only he knows the way out. Only he knows how to work this for our good. Only he can make treasures out of our turmoil. Only he can change our ruin into rejoicing. Only he can make diamonds out of our disaster. Only he can bring rubies from the rubbish and turn our tears into triumph. And only when we let him, can he use the evil attacks upon our lives and hearts and for our growth and his glory.

Badwater experiences are relieved by Living Water Springs. Desolation Canyon days give way to Divine Intervention. Our own Furnace Creeks no longer run dry, but overflow with the Rivers of Life. Our Black Mountain challenges glitter under the light of the Bright and Morning Star. Personal Funeral Mountains submit to Resurrection Morning!

Why? Because we are women of destiny and purpose, women of God—maturing, growing, and being guided by the hand of Almighty God. Because even the most devastating crisis and destructive situation can be used by God for my good and his glory. Death Valley detours can become places of soul restoration because of one eternal fact: "I belong to him, and he belongs to me." And that changes everything—forever.

The Bible says, "The crucible for silver and the furnace for gold, but the Lord tests the heart" (Prv 17:3). Death Valley detours test the heart—if we allow it.

"See, I have refined you, though not as silver; I have tested you in the furnace of affliction" (Is 48:10). Will we choose to be refined and purified?

"I will refine them like silver and test them like gold. They will call on my name and I will answer them; I will say 'They are my people,' and they will say, 'The Lord is our God'" (Zec 13:9). How much do we want to know God? Enough to let him test and refine us until we're pure?

Leonard Ravenhill writes these words:

Gold tried in a fire is of greater value than gold which still has a mixture of alloys. Gold that is shaped into an ornament has yet more value. Of still higher worth is gold purified, then shaped into a vessel, and finally beautifully engraved.

Even so in a believer's life. The cleansed Christian—purged of all self-interest, self-glory, self-pity, self-projection—is of great value to God. Yet there is a maturity beyond this, eloquent in some by its presence, but conspicuous in others by its absence. A head stuffed with theology or even stuffed with Bible verses is no substitute for the deep things of God worked out in us by the Spirit.

Regeneration is a birth; sanctification, on the other hand, is a death … we want to go *to* the cross, but few want to get *on* the cross. We want Christ to die *for us,* but we do not want to die *with him.* Christianity is all right if I can use it to my own ends. But when Christ wants to purge my squirming ego, crucify my stubborn self-will, eliminate my reeking self-pity, vanquish my vacillation, and reign supreme within the heart that he has purged—that is another matter.

Let the Christian's self-will be put to death by being crucified with Christ. Then by God's given grace, let him abide in Christ. This puts a Christian on the road to victory.

Only after death shall I be out of his [Satan's] range; though, thank God, I can be out of his power right now here and now. What Satan wants is for *his* power to work through *my* power against *God's* power. But God wants *his* power to swallow up *my* power so that "the power of Christ may rest upon me," and I may fight against principalities and powers.[1]

We have asked God to help us grow into women of strength.

To answer our prayer, to do the necessary work, he will use the circumstances of our lives to accomplish what he sees we need. He will leave no stone unturned that would cause us to stumble and fall. He will invite us to the cross. Not just to admire it, nor be thankful for it, but to get *on* it. The Death Valley detours that life throws at us, my friend, are our chance to see not only what he's made of, but the stuff we're made of. It gives us a chance to see life from the death-position on the cross of Christ.

No longer content to just get by, or get out, or even just to survive, aspiring women of strength choose to *grow* through the hardest times, the hottest furnace experiences, and the deadliest valleys that life offers.

We're learning what it actually means to be an overcomer. To let God search our hearts when we'd rather hide; to let him probe deeper when we want to curl up in a shell; to give him access to our raw emotions and excruciating pain; to believe that this will work for our good, when all the evidence points to defeat; to hope when there is no reason in sight to hope; to keep praying when we see no answers; to love him, even when he's silent.

Like Gordon MacDonald says, "It may be a time for the wilderness. But it is not a time for fear. Even though the pain might be great, life on the other end will be full of hope."[2]

David said it like this:

Even though I walk through the valley of the shadow of death, I will fear no evil, for you are with me; your rod and your staff, they comfort me. You prepare a table before me in the presence of my enemies. You anoint my head with oil; my cup overflows. Surely goodness and love will follow me all the days of my life, and I will dwell in the house of the LORD forever.   PSALM 23

Death Valley detours and the bitterness of life do not have to undo us. We are becoming women of strength. Victory is ours no matter how long and desperate the conflict or crisis. In the same way the snowcapped Paramint mountains rise far above Death Valley, California, so too, our spirits can rise above our deeply hurt, folded, twisted, and broken lives.

Our very lives are built on the promises of God.

Blessed is the [woman] who perseveres under trial, because when [she] has stood the test, [she] will receive the crown of life that God has promised to those who love him.

JAMES 1:12

Women of strength are destined for the crown of life. The God who is faithful to his promises has promised.

Milestone Markers

Nothing can sabotage a growing woman of strength faster than lethargy. After establishing a regular devotional life, learning the lessons of problem pass, being comfortable with a disciplined life, and then taking on the desert and coming through, who could blame her for just resting a bit?

Subtle thoughts of having "paid your dues," having life in order and under control, will set you up for unseen traps and strategies for the destruction of even more growth. No snare for a growing woman of strength is quite as effective as the thought, "I've made it, now it's time to relax." Such interior loafing can only lead to spiritual laziness. Would you really want to come this far and make such wonderful growth toward strength and then lose ground, simply because you loosened your grip and neglected to *grow* on, even from here?

✓ Checkpoint:

Think back to the most recent crisis in your life, then think back to the first one you can remember. How did you respond differently to each?

Did your differing responses reflect growth or merely experience? Discuss the difference.

How have you seen God work even difficult things together for your good?

Relate a time when you definitely experienced a "divine intervention." Was that a positive or negative experience?

How are you building your life on God's promises?

How does your life change when you hope even when there's no obvious reason to do so?

How do you change when you hope beyond reason to hope?

18

Eagle Rock Lookout

"Just show me what to do, Lord, and I'll do it!" How deeply I felt those words as I cried out to God during a Death Valley detour. "I'm a survivor," I reminded myself. "I'll climb my way out, if I have to."

I can't really tell you the exact day, nor even the decisive circumstance when I found Eagle Rock Lookout. Perhaps it took years and many Death Valley detour experiences before I learned the principle of Isaiah 40:31.

> Those who hope in the LORD will renew their strength. They will soar on wings like eagles....

You see, you don't climb or crawl your way out of Death Valley detours, you *wait* your way out.

Wait?

Yes, wait.

Oh, don't get me wrong here. We're not talking about denial, pretending that the Death Valley detour doesn't exist. Nor are we neglecting our situation through procrastination. We're talking about the Bible kind of waiting: actively, purposely, decisively waiting on God.

Those of us who have walked through enough of life and its difficulties know about circumstances so difficult that we've been left with seared imprints of failure and pain on our hearts. These are Death Valley detours that fill our minds with agonizing memories and sour thoughts. We are tired of being bound by the tortured thinking and distorted views caused by our dysfunctional lives and unfortunate experiences. Wanting to put all the pieces of our lives and souls together once again, we begin to search for answers to the ceaseless, inward questions. Trying to find peace from the painful doubts hammering away inside our minds, we're tempted to listen to advice to *work through it*, certainly not *wait* our way through it. How can we? We've seen too much, witnessed too much, experienced too much pain to just sit here, passively waiting for God to do something.

But, I'm not suggesting *passive* waiting for God. I'm promoting *active, deliberate, resolute waiting* on God. That means choosing to hope in him; choosing to believe in him; choosing to trust him at a level that defies whatever anguish we feel; choosing to watch for his intervention, exercising a faith in God that transcends the reality of our bereft and desolate situation.

I am suggesting electing to submit to God when we'd rather fight; deciding to remain calm, depending on him when it's more natural to be stressed out; choosing security in him, rather than the insecurity of whatever reality demands; selectively choosing satisfaction in him rather than the disappointment dictated by a Death Valley detour.

Believe it or not, it all happens when we take time to stop at *Eagle Rock Lookout*. There we lift our eyes from the white-hot flames of our most difficult experience to the blue skies of his grace. Sometimes we find we can't do anything about our situation, and we shouldn't—even if we could. Yes, we're becoming women of strength, learning to wait on God. We're choosing to leave ourselves in his hands, entirely. We take our hands off and abandon our solution-based nature. It isn't easy, but it can be done.

And suddenly, there they are, up high, circling above: eagles. High above the valley floor, they have learned to stretch their wings, catch the updrafts, and soar. That's the word-picture promise given to those of us who learn to wait in hope upon the Lord.

It's because of Death Valley detours we come to grips with the depth of our faith—the strength of our hope. God leads us from the depths of Death Valley to the heights of Eagle Rock Lookout and there we realize something: those Death Valley detours are where our beliefs move from the test-lab of theory into the proven reality of life. This is how sturdy Christians become heavy-duty Christians. And we find again through our experience that God will never let us down—*no matter what!*

There are no short cuts to becoming a woman of strength. No formulas to follow to make it easier. But there is no doubt in my mind that if we are ever going to become women of strength, the guesswork of being a Christian has to be eliminated. The characteristics of authenticity will be unlocked and we will learn strength through *waiting* our way out of our Death Valley detours.

It's not a stay-here-and-rest kind of waiting. Not some sort of spiritual or emotional loitering and hanging around until something changes. No. This kind of waiting keeps us in faithful anticipation, hopeful expectation, and a trustful counting on God like never before. We wait while watching for his hand in every situation; looking for his stamp of approval upon every possible solution; keeping a sharp eye out for him as we wait.

Waiting, watching, hoping—all that and more. Waiting and ready to live in faith-filled readiness, available to him as much as he's made himself available to us. Even in the most difficult situation, we must be reserved for God and God alone.

And how is this waiting done? Let the Bible give you the answer.

Lift Up Your Soul

To you, O LORD, I lift up my soul; in you I trust, O my God. Do not let me be put to shame, nor let my enemies triumph over me. No one whose hope is in you will ever be put to shame, but they will be put to shame who are treacherous without excuse. Show me your ways, O LORD, teach me your paths; guide me in your truth and teach me, for you are God my Savior, and my hope is in you all day long. PSALMS 25:1-5

Look for God's Face

Hear my voice when I call, O LORD; be merciful to me and answer me. My heart says of you, "Seek his face!" Your face, LORD, I will seek. Do not hide your face from me, do not turn your servant away in anger; you have been my helper. Do not reject me or forsake me, O God my Savior. Though my father and mother forsake me, the LORD will receive me.

PSALMS 27:7-10

Look for Lessons in Troubled Times

Teach me your way, O LORD; lead me in a straight path because of my oppressors. Do not turn me over to the desire of my foes, for false witnesses rise up against me, breathing out violence.

PSALMS 27:11-12

Look for the Goodness of God

I am still confident of this: I will see the goodness of the LORD in the land of the living.   PSALMS 27:13

Look to the Hand of the Master

As the eyes of slaves look to the hand of their master, as the eyes of a maid look to the hand of her mistress, so our eyes look to the LORD our God, till he shows us his mercy.   PSALMS 123:2

Look for the Lord's Deliverance

I waited patiently for the LORD; he turned to me and heard my cry. He lifted me out of the slimy pit, out of the mud and mire; he set my feet on a rock and gave me a firm place to stand. He put a new song in my mouth, a hymn of praise to our God. Many will see and fear and put their trust in the LORD. Blessed is the man who makes the LORD his trust.   PSALMS 40:1-4

Look for Strength

O LORD, be gracious to us; we long for you. Be our strength every morning, our salvation in time of distress.   ISAIAH 33:2

When was the last time you actually lifted up your soul to the Lord? When you were happy? When was a prayer answered or a need met? How about in a Death Valley detour experience? Did you lift your soul to the Lord then? I've found that it's almost easier when there is nothing else I can do, no way out, no hope or energy left. Then, I feel compelled to cry out to God and to "wait upon the Lord." In fact, isn't it in Death Valley detours where we learn to do just that?

Waiting on the Lord is not really that much different than stopping at the edge of a vista point on some highway to take in the view. The difference is that this vista point is in your heart—right where you are, in whatever life has handed you this very moment. Go ahead, close your eyes. Lift up your soul.

Even when circumstances deliver the most distressing emotions, the deepest pain, and the future seems darkest, we can be confident in God's goodness. Though everything we believed in, trusted in, and hoped for be ripped from us, we can still be assured of God's love and care. "I will see," we can say with confidence. "Maybe I don't see it now, but I will. God's goodness is the one thing I can be confident in." I've found it to be true, how about you?

We're far more willing to be taught when everything is hunky-dory, right? "For goodness sake," we protest, "times of trouble and distress are no time to be learning lessons!" Right? Wrong! It's the perfect time. Stripped of our defenses, robbed of our self-sufficiency, barren of our self-confidence, this is the time we can be taught the best lessons and insights when we open our hearts to God.

Obedience is the expression—the acting out of our commitment to wait upon God in hope and trust. In a Death Valley detour experience it can be so easy to forget that we are servants and to become victims. Woman of God, arise. Take your rightful place as a servant of the Most High God. Look only to him for the mercy for which you long and that you need. He alone can lift you from your sorrow and exalt you to the position of his obedient, cherished child.

Look up! See how the eagle soars overhead. We don't need to claw or climb our way out of the Death Valley detour experiences of life, we can soar out. We *rise!* We wait and hope our way to new heights above it all.

"And God raised us up with Christ and seated us with him in the heavenly realms in Christ Jesus..." (Eph 2:6).

Woman of strength, look up! Then look back. From this perspective you can see that Death Valley detours weren't the end, they were the beginning. It was the waiting room for God's promises and provisions; the entrance into a new strength and vitality as a Christian woman; the receiving room of his grace in untold measures.

Strong Woman Pitfall Warning!

Could there really be a pitfall at this point in our lives? Most assuredly there is. There is a booby trap that even the most mature woman of strength must watch out for. It is assuming that my faith is what has brought me this far. It hasn't been *my* faith; it's *his* grace. Grace has brought me here, nothing but the unfailing grace of Almighty God. His matchless love and ever-sustaining power have been available to me just when I need them most. That's what has gotten me here safely. Faith is not a badge of honor or a kingdom-coupon to cash in. It's a response to what already exists. My faith doesn't create God, he creates it within me. Of course, women of strength have lots of faith. After all they've seen and experienced, they can't help but have faith. They also have God's grace. We need lots of it and, fortunately, he is gracious in abundance!

✓ Checkpoint:

Are you most likely to respond to Death Valley detours by crawling and climbing your way out or stopping at Eagle Rock Lookout and "faith-waiting" your way out?

Why is waiting so incredibly hard?

When was the last time you decidedly waited on God, even though it was in your power to choose a more active solution?

How do you watch faithfully for his intervention or involvement in the situations in your life?

How does this strengthen you?

How does our American tendency for "hurry" get in your way of prayer?

How does our ability for quick answers and solutions hinder faith and growth?

What would you like to see happen in your growth in prayer and faith?

How could God answer that prayer?

19

Powerhouse Point

I hear the question. "Are we there yet?"

Almost. We're nearly *there*. As long as this trip has been, you are about to see the most wonderful point of it all—the emergence of a woman of strength.

Growing on with our lives, whether it be away from mere dissatisfaction, devastating pasts, or pain-filled failures takes time, and it takes effort. But eventually we'll be the women of strength we'd prayed to become. We will be women who are confident of the abilities God has given each one of us; assured of our potential; satisfied we have the right stuff to do and be what it takes to live as women of great inner strength and Christlike character; women whose influence for Christ goes beyond the limits of our talents and gifts. Women who are dependent upon what God can do in a heart fully surrendered to him. We are becoming women whose sense of personal worth and value to the kingdom of God is no longer based on self or other-imposed limitations or culturally-determined gender barriers. We are on the threshold of becoming women of strength—women who are stepping into their full destinies as women of God.

We are becoming powerhouse people. We've reclaimed our lives—past, present, and future. We've decided to snatch back that which has been stolen from us by victimizers and abusers. And in the process, we are changing from the inside out.

Our new inner strength gives us renewed energy. It gives us a deep inner vitality and we can sense a new fortitude because of our choice to *grow* into his strength. Rounding a significant corner, we have power like we've never had before.

Power to Love

Romans 8:35-39 says:

Who shall separate us from the love of Christ? Shall trouble or hardship or persecution or famine or nakedness or danger or sword? As it is written: "For your sake we face death all day long; we are considered as sheep to be slaughtered." No, in all these things we are more than conquerors through him who loved us. For I am convinced that neither death nor life, neither angels nor demons, neither the present nor the future, nor any powers, neither height nor depth, nor anything else in all creation, will be able to separate us from the love of God that is in Christ Jesus our Lord.

In the last several chapters, we have looked at some of life's most difficult circumstances. We have chosen to react differently to their threats and respond differently to God as we give him our trust. We have actually tasted the reality of what Romans 8:35-39 is all about. We have not only read the words of the Bible, but have made a purposeful decision to *experience* them. And, standing at Powerhouse Point, we are aware of the power to love, and have the freedom to love, because we now know he loves us *through* our most difficult places. He loves us *through* the deepest pain, *through* our most troubling days.

Now let us walk in the power of his love and share it with others, too. "My command is this," Jesus says in John 15:12, "Love each other as I have loved you."

Power to Forgive

The pathway from the past into the future while becoming women of strength is not without its challenges and difficulties. You may have experienced anything from small setbacks to major defeats during this time. You may have decided to let other women finish this trek, feeling as though the challenges presented here were just too overwhelming. But life happens to you anyway, doesn't it? So why not make the most of it? Why let the ruination of life ruin you? Forgive yourself for straying or taking some wrong turn along the line. You can get to Powerhouse Point, too. You'd be surprised how fast you can get back on track with the one simple act of forgiving yourself.

Then, the Bible says, "Be kind and compassionate to one another, forgiving each other, just as in Christ God forgave you" (Eph 4:32).

Women like you and me who have chosen to let God use our pain-filled pasts and failures to make us into women of strength must come to the powerhouse of forgiveness. What joy it is to forgive those who have wronged us, who have abused us, who have limited us and kept us back! What power it gives us to free ourselves from such destruction through forgiveness! The deepest parts of our inner selves—our hearts and souls that have been consumed by unforgiveness—are remade. We are women of freedom and forgiveness.

Power to Decide

When we become women of strength we discover the power in Christ to decide who and what we will become and to what we will give ourselves. With our lives based firmly on God's love and knowing the wholeness of his redemption, we choose more carefully now. And we have the power to decide—we are women of "the made-up mind."

As women of strength, we choose life according to Deuteronomy 30:19. We choose to serve God and God alone (Joshua 24:15). We choose the understanding of Proverbs 16:16. We choose to believe we are chosen women because of John 15:16. And we can decide for ourselves to choose to do God's will (John 7:17).

Power to Grow

Say to yourself, "Since nothing in all creation can separate and keep me from the love of God, then nothing can deter my growth in him. With God's power, I can *grow* through every circumstance, every situation, every one of life's severest blows and tests. Because of him I have grown through problems, desert places, and Death Valley detour experiences."

Power to Heal

In addition to the wonderful growth you have experienced in your own journey getting from *here* to *there,* you also have the power to bring that wonderful healing and growth to others. Look around. Don't you know at least one other woman who has the potential to become a woman of strength? You have the power to help her find the healing, purpose, and wholeness she'll need. All women of strength have this power. They need to ask others to join them as they progress in their walk with God.

Power to Overcome

As a growing woman of strength, you have more power to overcome than you ever realized. You see, that's what the problems, the dry places, and the Death Valley experiences have shown you. You couldn't see it then, you were just getting through—but now, here at Powerhouse Point, let the memories of those experiences generate the energy in you that you'll need as you *grow* on from here.

Power to Follow Christ

When we determine to become women of strength, we determine to follow Christ. And, when we make that choice, we soon realize that his pathway is a pathway of challenge and suffering. Looking back, we can see that we suffer in this life no matter what, and realize that this is the Calvary road. "Take up [your] cross daily," Jesus urges, "and follow me" (Luke 9:23). "Yes, Lord," we reply. "I *will* follow you."

Power to Pray from a "Changing" Perspective

Once a woman begins to see life from the perspective of becoming a woman of strength, her prayers change, don't they? Mine have. When I keep my mind set on becoming a woman of strength, even the words I choose for my prayers are different. Instead of, "Oh, Lord, get me through this," I find myself praying, "Oh, Lord, what do you want me to learn in this?" Rather than, "Dear God, change this," I more frequently pray, "Dear God, change me because of this."

Power to Believe Again

If you and I would take the time to think about it, we'd realize that our lives are memorials to strength, survival, and even to the miraculous power and grace of God. Looking over my shoulder I can see the highway of my life littered with the trash of my own efforts, my failures, and my discarded hopes and dreams. But there is still a road ahead. I'm still living and breathing, and so are you.

At this momentary stop at Powerhouse Point, remind yourself that we are still *growing*. We're not quite *there*, that's true. But let's at least breathe an inward "Hallelujah" that we've come so far. Even though we've not quite arrived, we certainly are well on our way.

However, before we traverse much further, I need to warn you that dangerous curves are always ahead. No matter how old we get, no matter that we're in the process of becoming, if we're not careful, we can fall headlong into the pitfalls of becoming strong women, not the women of strength God wants us to be.

Another Strong Woman Pitfall Warning?

By now I may not even need to remind you with a Strong Woman Pitfall Warning. I would, however, tell you that's the most important warning of all.

You see, when you and I assume that we've grown so far, come through so much, and learned all there is to learn, we're in grave danger. If we ever let ourselves even begin to entertain thoughts that we're untouchable, undeceivable, and that our course never needs correction, we're more likely to be deceived and may be in need of correction more than ever before.

We're growin' to the very end. We're growin' the distance. We're growin' all the way. And friend, we're all growin' together!

✓ Checkpoint:

How has this book served you in your desire to grow in Christ?

What parts have been the easiest to accept?

The most difficult?

Which have caused you to think the most?

To search your heart?

What did you read that made you the most angry?

Have you changed since reading this book? How did it come about?

20

Women of Strength– Where Do We Go from Here?

I urge you to view life from the perspective that absolutely nothing comes to us without God's knowledge. Such a perspective helps us make trophies from the trash of our lives. It helps us make sense and triumph of senseless tragedies. It lifts us above the deep valleys painfully carved in our minds and souls. It gives us the courage to not only survive the pain and challenges of our existence, but to rise above them in such a way as to inspire and benefit others in the process.

A renewed perspective emerges daily from within each of us, based on God's love and compassion for us. Our experiences can now deepen our characters instead of robbing us of ourselves.

Seize Your Present

This is the day when you and I can begin to walk and talk like the women of strength we were designed to be, to live as women of faith, courage, and accomplishment that no person, present situation, or past experience can deny or suppress any longer. Yes, today is the day.

You and I stand at a threshold of promise, of purpose, and of value. This is a pivotal place between yesterday and tomorrow. We are standing today on the footbridge to our future. Today is ours, yours and mine—and it's the only time given to us to make the changes necessary to live victoriously. This is the only time given to us to determine to grow—this moment, this day.

Search Your Heart

After reading this book, you may feel the need to examine your heart. I urge you to do so. Turn in your "stuck-in-my-problems" philosophy for a new "I-can-do-all-things-through-Christ" attitude. Adopt a new way of looking at life through eyes of faith—not because of what you haven't done or experienced, but because of what you have! Have faith in the God who has brought you this far. Faith that he will lead you on still farther. Faith that he can use you, not only in spite of what you have been through, but even more so *because* of what you've been through. Faith that he will make something of worth and purpose out of what you consider worthless and of no value at all.

Search your heart. Find any attitude that keeps you focused on your situation rather than God's provision. Uncover the excuses you've used to keep you down and bound, and expose them to the light of God's Word and promises of hope and love. Dislodge joy-robbing justifications for your negativity; put joy-filled truth in their place. Root out unhealthy defenses, tear down the self-erected barriers that keep out God's love and purpose for your life.

Give the devil the boot and open the windows of your soul for a fresh breath of God's holy love.

Then, just when you think you've got it all out, open wider and let God examine your whole heart. Let him look behind the dressers where you've stored all your painful memories. Invite him to look into the closets of your soul and the crannies of your wide-open heart. Pray the prayer of Psalms 139:23-24: "Search me, O God, and know my heart; test me and know my anxious thoughts. See if there is any offensive way in me, and lead me in the way everlasting."

Sanctify Your Mind

Get rid of what motivational speakers call "stinkin' thinkin'." You are a child of God, an emerging woman of strength. Pray the prayer of Psalms 139:1-4.

O LORD, you have searched me and you know me. You know when I sit and when I rise; you perceive my thoughts from afar. You discern my going out and my lying down; you are familiar with all my ways. Before a word is on my tongue you know it completely, O LORD.

And pray with the psalmist Psalms 19:14: "May the words of my mouth and the meditation of my heart be pleasing in your sight, O LORD, my Rock and my Redeemer."

Determine that you will follow the words of Romans 12:2: "Do not conform any longer to the pattern of this world, but be transformed by the renewing of your mind." Let this become a reality in your life.

Today is the day that with thoroughly searched hearts and renewed minds, we will take decisive action and open our minds to truth, love, peace, purpose, and worth. We will close them against destruction, defeat, and despair.

We have a *woman of strength* mind-set now. The godly strength of the sanctified mind is ours.

Secure Your Future

No longer dependent on experiences for our validation, our futures have never looked brighter. Not only does our outlook change, but our "in-look" as well. Our talk changes. Words of hope and optimism spring from hope-filled hearts. Words of purpose and destiny pour from our whole and healthy attitudes. We are changing before the very eyes of those who thought we'd never be different. We are healing in spite of the forces bent on our destruction. The defeater is defeated. No longer a threat to our lives and destinies, our personally assigned Rumplestiltskin has heard his name called out loud and clear, and he stamps his way into oblivion in a temper tantrum.

Women of strength, we talk a faith talk and walk an obedient walk. Today is the time when we choose to lay claim to our future. We choose to be women of strength—a decision that nobody else can make for us, nor can they prevent us from making it.

Our secured futures lie before us. Today is the first step of our journey with a destiny no longer tainted by the threat of yesterday's defeats and failures; we look into a mirror and see the face of a brand new me in the making—the real me, a never ending story.

Epilogue

My friend, you and I have undertaken quite a journey together. I can't begin to tell you how honored I feel that you have read this book and have taken the steps with me toward becoming a woman of strength.

No other book I have ever written has challenged me to the depths of my own soul and caused me to search my own heart as much as this one. I can't recall any writing project that has driven me to my knees, brought tears to my eyes, and caused me to cry out to God as much as this one has.

I owe a special debt of gratitude to Gwen Ellis, my outstanding editor who also became my friend during this project. Thank you, Gwen, for believing in me, this message, and for seeing the value and hope it will bring to the women for whom it was written.

Special thanks to my friends Judy, Beth, and Denise, who kept me encouraged in the months it took to explore, then write these concepts. Thanks to friends who lovingly prodded me through the tough parts of writing this book.

Also, I need to thank my daughter, Rhonda, a remarkable young woman who is taking giant, courageous steps out of her own pain-filled experiences into new spiritual depth and strength.

And who, in her own way, challenges me to keep growing as well.

And, more than they can ever know, I appreciate and thank the women on both the East and West Coasts who met with me in focus groups to willingly give their valuable perspectives and insight. I count it a personal privilege to have discussed these issues with them. I was amazed at how open and generous each woman was with her heartfelt thoughts and personal experiences. All of us came away with a deep inner knowing that we had touched on something that had the power to change our lives. Many commented to me that they would never look at themselves or other women quite the same way again.

None of us will ever be able to say, "I've made it! I'm a woman of strength!" But how encouraging to know that we are getting there—*growing* on with our lives to become what God intended we become. I wish I could give you a nice shiny button to wear after reading this book, a colorful one with bright letters. This button would say to the whole world: "Here is one who is becoming a WOMAN OF STRENGTH!" And I'd give the very first one to my special friend and mentor, Barb Tollefson.

Notes

TWO
"How'd I Get Here, Anyway?"

1. Psalms 139:13: "For you created my inmost being; you knit me together in my mother's womb."
2. John 10:10: "I have come that they may have life, and have it to the full."

THREE
Abigail—A Woman of Strength

1. See Abigail's story in 1 Samuel 25.

FOUR
Who Are They, These Women of Strength?

1. All examples used in this chapter are based on the reference material in Herbert Lockyer's wonderful book, *All the Women in the Bible* (Grand Rapids, Mich.: Zondervan, 1988).

2. David Hazard, *Majestic Is Your Name, A 40-Day Journey in the Company of Teresa of Avila* (Minneapolis: Bethany House, 1993), 7,8.
3. Elisabeth Elliot, *A Chance to Die: The Life and Legacy of Amy Carmichael* (Old Tappan, N.J.: Revell, 1987), 328.
4. Nancy A. Hardesty, *Great Women of Faith* (Grand Rapids, Mich.: Baker, 1980), 13.

FIVE
The Stuff of Which Women of Strength Are Made

1. Esther 4:14.
2. Luke 10:38-42.

SEVEN
Rebekah—A Strong Woman

1. Rebekah's story begins in Genesis 24.

NINE
Where Exactly, Is There?

1. 1 Peter 2:9 "But you are a chosen people, a royal priesthood, a holy nation, a people belonging to God...."
2. 2 Corinthians 5:20: "We are therefore Christ's ambassadors, as though God were making his appeal through us."
3. Isaiah 53:9.
4. Isaiah 50:4.

TEN
Mentors—Close Encounters of the Strengthening Kind

1. Ruth 2-4.
2. Luke 1:42-56.

ELEVEN
Quiet Time Square

1. Stephen D. Eyre, *Quiet Time Dynamics* (Downers Grove, Ill.: PathFinder Pamphlets, InterVarsity Press, 1989), 4.
2. Henri Nouwen, *The Way of the Heart* (San Francisco: Harper and Row, 1981), 30.
3. Gordon MacDonald, *Ordering Your Private World* (Nashville: Oliver Nelson, Thomas Nelson, 1985), 123.
4. Henri J. Nouwen, *With Burning Hearts* (Maryknoll, N.Y.: Orbis, 1994), 70.
5. Jack Hayford, *Encylopedia of Prayer Tape and Study Set* (Sherman Oaks, Calif.: Living Way Ministries, 1996) tape 10, study guide, 11.
6. Thomas H. Green, *Opening to God* (Notre Dame, Ind.: Ave Maria Press, 1977), 89.
7. John 16:13.
8. Jack Hayford, *Moments with Majesty* (Portland, Ore.: Multnomah, 1990), back cover.
9. Matthew 4:4.
10. Hayford, *Moments with Majesty,* back cover.
11. Nouwen, *The Way of the Heart,* 76.

TWELVE
Prayer Pulloff

1. *The Complete Works of E.M. Bounds on Prayer* (Grand Rapids, Mich.: Baker, 1990), 17.

THIRTEEN
Discipline Drive

1. Galatians 5:22-23.
2. Dale Hanson Bourke, "Making Those Dreams Come True," *Today's Christian Woman*, September/October 1984, 40.
3. Jerry Bridges, *The Pursuit of Holiness* (Colorado Springs: NavPress, 1978), 42.

FOURTEEN
Reclamation Road

1. Larry Crabb, *Inside Out* (Colorado Springs: NavPress, 1988), 103.
2. David Seamands, *Putting Away Childish Things* (Wheaton, Ill.: Victor, 1982), 28.
3. David Seamands, *Healing of Memories* (Wheaton, Ill.: Victor, 1985), 31.

FIFTEEN
Problem Pass

1. Neva Coyle, *Making Sense of Pain and Struggle* (Minneapolis: Bethany House, 1992), 19.

SIXTEEN
The Desert Crossing

1. Matthew 4:1.
2. Genesis 16:7; Genesis 21:17.
3. Psalms 139:7-8.
4. Exodus 3:4.
5. 1 Kings 19:9-13.
6. Hosea 2:14-15.
7. 1 Samuel 23:14; Psalm 55:6-8.
8. 1 Kings 19:4.
9. Isaiah 35:8-9.
10. Isaiah 43:20-21.
11. John 6:32-35.

SEVENTEEN
Detour Through Death Valley

1. Leonard Ravenhill, *Tried and Transfigured* (Minneapolis: Bethany House, 1963), 63, 64, 137, 140.
2. Gordon MacDonald, *Rebuilding Your Broken World* (Nashville: Oliver Nelson, 1988), 181.

Women of Confidence

S E R I E S

The Women of Confidence Series is designed to help women confidently express their God-given gifts in every facet of their intellect, personality, style, and talents. All women have things they wish they could do better—or do at all. Those things may be something practical and close to home—like learning to communicate or to entertain. Or they could be something to fortify the soul—like praying. From helping women define personal goals and build strong relationships, to learning how to communicate and deepen their spirituality, this series has it all.

Written by respected Christian communicators and authors, the Women of Confidence Series helps women find new ways to live enthusiastically and confidently in the light of God's love.